Thrive! – All Thrive Forever®

What Will You Do? ® The Game. The Challenge.

by

Gary "Chris" Christopherson

Founder, *Thrive!*® - Building a Thriving Future
Founder, HealthePeople® - Building a Healthy and Thriving Future

Nelson, WI   University Park, MD

ISBN- 13: 978-1512387414

ISBN-10: 151238741X

DEDICATION

People who help build, achieve and sustain
a surviving and thriving future for all forever.

Irene and Lynn Christopherson, nurturing and inspiring parents.
Dr. Patricia Haeuser, friend and supporter.

TRADEMARKS *[by Gary A. Christopherson]*

Thrive!®

Thrive! Endeavor®

T!®

All Thrive Forever®

What will you do?®

HealthePeople®

Public advocacy to promote awareness of the need for positive and integrative decision-making in the fields of public policy, public administration, healthcare and healthcare reform for the purpose of creating and sustaining positive change and a better, thriving future for communities on the local, state, regional and national levels

Note to Reader

In electronic eBook versions of *Thrive!* – **All Thrive Forever** all hyperlinks are active for navigating within the eBook and navigating to the Internet.

About The Author

[TOC]

Gary (Chris) Christopherson continues to work nationally and locally on improving health, reducing vulnerability and building a better future. Currently, he develops strategy, management and policy for creating, managing and sustaining large positive change and building a better and thriving future for all forever. ThrivingFuture.org He wrote the nonfiction books **Thrive! - Building a Thriving Future, Thrive! - People's Guide to a Thriving Future, Thrive! – All Thrive Forever, The Thrive! Philosophy** and **Thrive! Endeavor** available via Amazon.com and ThrivingFuture.org.

Thrive! draws on his 30+ years experience creating, managing and sustaining large positive change at national and local levels in public and private sectors. He founded **HealthePeople** (building a healthy and thriving future; HealthePeople.com), *via***Future** (creating large positive change) and **Vulnerable** (minimizing vulnerability). He served as a senior leader, manager and policymaker responsible for multi-billion dollar policy, programs and budgets and thousands of employees. His public service includes: Principal Deputy Assistant Secretary and Acting Assistant Secretary of Defense for Health Affairs and Senior Advisor, Department of Defense; Associate Director, Presidential Personnel, Executive Office of the President, White House; Senior Fellow, National Academy of Public Administration; Senior Advisor to Chief Operating Officer and Deputy Director for the Quality Improvement Group, Centers for Medicare and Medicaid Services, DHHS; Senior Advisor to Under Secretary, Veterans Health Administration, VA; Senior Fellow and Scholar-In-Residence, Institute of Medicine, National Academy of Sciences; Chief Information Officer, Veterans Health Administration, VA; Director of Health Legislation, House Select Committee on Aging, U.S. House of Representatives.

He is a sculptor of abstract art, focusing on Thrive! sculptures and creating over 150 sculptures. GChris Sculpture at GChris.com. He wrote science fiction novel **black box** and illustrated children's book **Angel, Thriving Creator of Artful Things**. Both are available via Amazon.com and GChris.com.

He received his bachelor's in political science and his master's in urban and regional planning from the University of Wisconsin – Madison, and did doctoral work in health policy and management at John Hopkins University School of Public Health.

Thrive! – All Thrive Forever

What Will You Do? ® The Game. The Challenge.

Thrive! – All Thrive Forever
What Will You Do? ® The Game. The Challenge.

Table of Contents

Brief Summary
[TOC]

"Thrive! – All Thrive Forever" is like a strategic video game that is not a game and not (yet) a video game. Not fantasy, it is todays and future reality. Even if you choose not to play, the "game" goes on with real-life consequences for you and for whom and what you care about. It may be played as just a strategic video game (or simulation) or as a strategic video "game" that is real-life played in real-time with real people, including you with real consequences. Real-life "enemies" stop you, your community and/or the world from surviving and thriving. Real-life friends help you survive and thrive. During play, you and all of us face four possible futures: Current, Survive, Partial Thrive, and Full Thrive. To win, you must get past Current and Survive. Real-life win is surviving <u>and</u> thriving in the real world. Ultimate real-life win, via the Thrive Endeavor, is Full Thrive where "all thrive forever" in the real world. At beginning of "play" is issued the challenge – "What will you do [to thrive]? You choose simulation or real-life mode. You choose your "game" – 1) you for yourself, 2) you and your community for your community) or 3) the Thrive Endeavor (you and all of us now and future) for the world+ so "all thrive forever". Then you "play" **Thrive!**. [Web version @ ThriveForever.org]

Summary
[TOC]

"Thrive! – All Thrive Forever" is like a strategic video game that is not a game and not (yet) a video game. Not fantasy, it is todays and future reality. Even if you choose not to play, the "game" goes on with real-life consequences for you and for whom and what you care about. It may be played as just a strategic video game (or simulation) or as a strategic video "game" that is real-life played in real-time with real people, including you with real consequences. Real-life "enemies" stop you, your community and/or the world from surviving and thriving. Real-life friends help you survive and thrive. Real-life win is surviving <u>and</u> thriving in the real world. Ultimate real-life win, via Thrive Endeavor, is "all thrive forever" in the real world.

At beginning of "play" is issued the challenge – "What will you do [to thrive]? You choose your "game" – 1) you for yourself, 2) you and your community for your community) or 3) the Thrive Endeavor (you and all of us now and future) so "all thrive forever". Then you "play" Thrive!. [Web version @ ThriveForever.org]

During "play", you and all of us face four possible futures:
- Current Path where there is little thriving and survival ends much too soon. Loss.
- Survive Path where there is little thriving and survival is extended but still ends too soon. Smaller loss.
- Partial Thrive Path where there is more thriving and survival is extended more but still ends too soon. Partial win.
- Full Thrive Path where there is high thriving and survival is extended to maximum. Ultimate win.

To avoid losing, get off Current Path. For ultimate win, get on Full Thrive Path where you and all of us survive and thrive today, near and far future, and forever.

This is "Thrive!".
- Game choice is simulation or real-life mode.
- Game choice is single-player (you for yourself), multiplayer (you and your community for your community), or ultimate massively multiplayer is Thrive Endeavor (you and all of us

now and future) for the world+ with ultimate win of "all thrive forever".

- Game Characters include you and simulation and/or real-life characters.
- Players engage together on strategy, tactics, logistics (resources), obstacles, internal/external changes, and action.
- Real-life enemies stop people from surviving and thriving. Real-life friends help you survive and thrive.
- Setting is your immediate environment, your community, or our world+ (world and beyond).
- Play map is drawn by players for play environment – single-player (your immediate environment now and future), multiplayer (your community(which can be friends, family, affinity group, local community, state, country, region) now and future), and the ultimate massively multiplayer (world+ forever).
- Exploration, before and during play, is of your ever-changing play environment (yourself and your immediate internal/external environment; yourself and your community and its internal/external environment; yourself and the world+ and its environment).
- Play is real-time - now, near and far future and forever.
- "Wins and losses" are for near and far future. Ultimate win is for forever. Wins and losses are real.

Play Thrive! real life, real-time with real people and real consequences. Score wins and losses with Thrive Scoresheet. Play to win thriving future!

0. How to "play" "Thrive! – All Thrive Forever". How to survive and thrive.
1. What will you do so you thrive?
   a. Single Player, Real-time
   b. Win – you survive and thrive today, near future, far future.
2. What will you and your community do so it thrives?
   a. Multiplayer, Real-time
   b. Win – you and your community survive and thrive today, near future, far future.
3. What will Thrive Endeavor (you and all of us) do for world+ so all thrive forever?

a. Ultimate Massively Multiplayer, Real-time, Late Game
b. Ultimate win - "all thrive forever"

0: How To "Play" "Thrive! – All Thrive Forever". How To Survive and Thrive. [1]

- What Will You Do [To Thrive]? The Challenge.

[Web version @ ThriveForever.org]

Getting Started

"Thrive! – All Thrive Forever" is like a strategic video game that is not a game and not (yet) a video game. Not fantasy, it is todays and future reality. [2] Even if you choose not to play, the "game" goes on with real-life consequences for you and for whom and what you care about. It plays like a strategic video game but is real-life played in real-time with real people, including you. Real-life "enemies" stop you, your community and/or the world from surviving and thriving. Real-life friends help you survive and thrive. Real-life win is surviving <u>and</u> thriving in the real world. Ultimate real-life win, via the Thrive Endeavor®, is Full Thrive where "all thrive forever®" in the real world. [See <u>Graphic - Thrive! – All Thrive Forever</u>]

---

[1] Thrive!® has several meanings:
- Thrive! is vision of a thriving and surviving future forever for all (our selves, family and friends, communities, countries and world).
- Thrive! is human aspiration to build, achieve and sustain a surviving and thriving future for all forever.
- Thrive! is mission to create and sustain large, positive and timely change that builds and achieves a surviving and thriving future for all forever.
- Thrive! is call to action and rallying cry to build, achieve and sustain a surviving and thriving future for all forever.
- Thrive! is vast Thrive! Endeavor by all of us to build, achieve and sustain a surviving and thriving future for all forever.

[2] Terms "game" and "play" are used but refers to real people, real life, real time and real consequences.

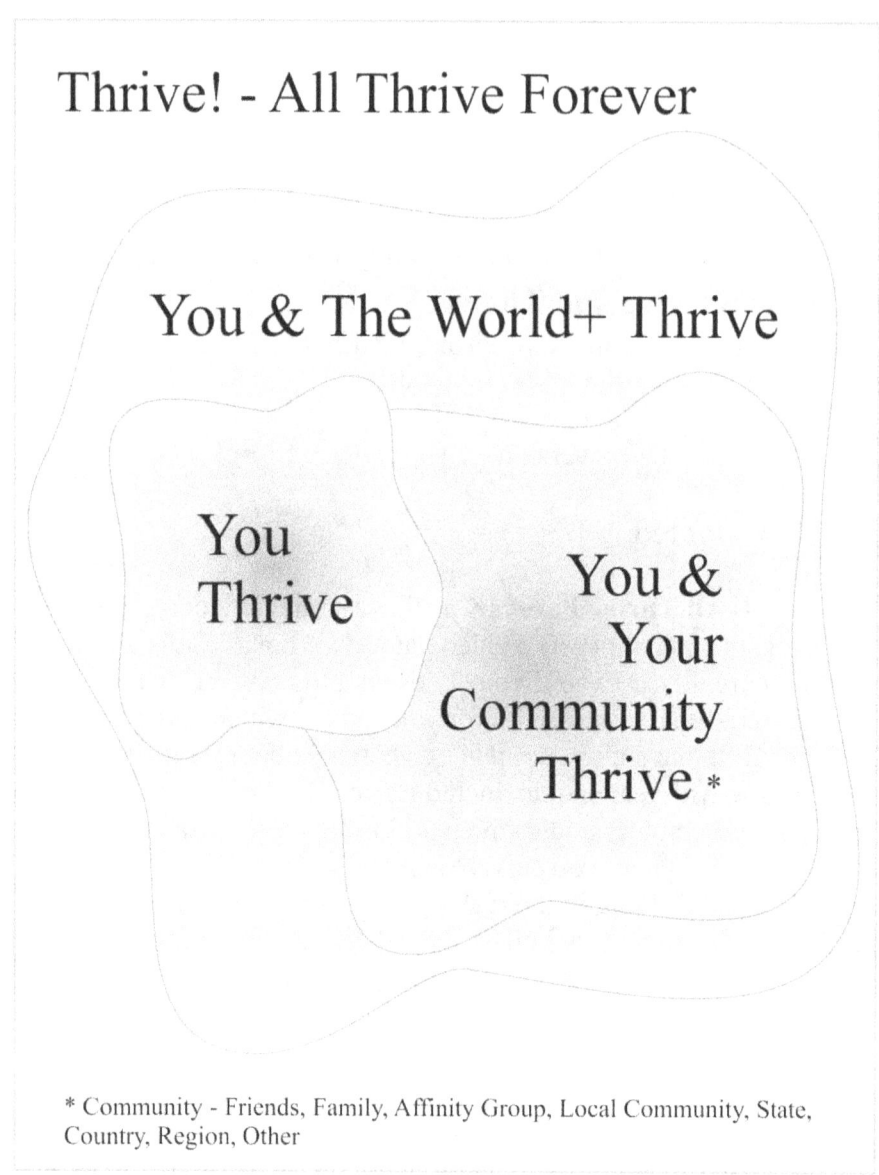

Thrive! - All Thrive Forever

You & The World+ Thrive

You
Thrive

You &
Your
Community
Thrive *

* Community - Friends, Family, Affinity Group, Local Community, State,
Country, Region, Other

Graphic - Thrive! - All Thrive Forever.

At beginning of "play" is issued the challenge – "What will you do [to thrive]? You choose your "game":

- You for yourself to thrive,
- You and your community for your community to thrive or
- The Thrive Endeavor (you and all of us now and future) for the world+ so "all thrive forever".

If you choose community, then choose whether it is friends, family, affinity group, local community, state, country or region.

During "play", you and all of us face four possible futures [See Graphic - Future for Surviving and Thriving]:

- Current Path where there is little thriving and survival ends much too soon. Loss.
- Survive Path where there is little thriving and survival is extended but still ends too soon. Smaller loss.
- Partial Thrive Path where there is more thriving and survival is extended more but still ends too soon. Partial win.
- Full Thrive Path where there is high thriving and survival is extended to maximum. Ultimate win.

To avoid losing, get off Current Path. For ultimate win, get on Full Thrive Path where you and all of us survive and thrive today, near and far future, and forever.

Strategy is to move from highly vulnerable and not surviving to surviving to highly thriving and has three elements [See Graphic - What will you do [to thrive]?]:

- Do what increases thriving.
- Do what prevents more vulnerability and survival threats.
- Do what reduces vulnerability and ensures survival.

Tactics and actions are determined by you and the other players.

Winning is measured by 1) how much vulnerability has been prevented and/or reduced and for how long, 2) has survival been ensured and for how long, and 3) how much thriving has been achieved and for how long.

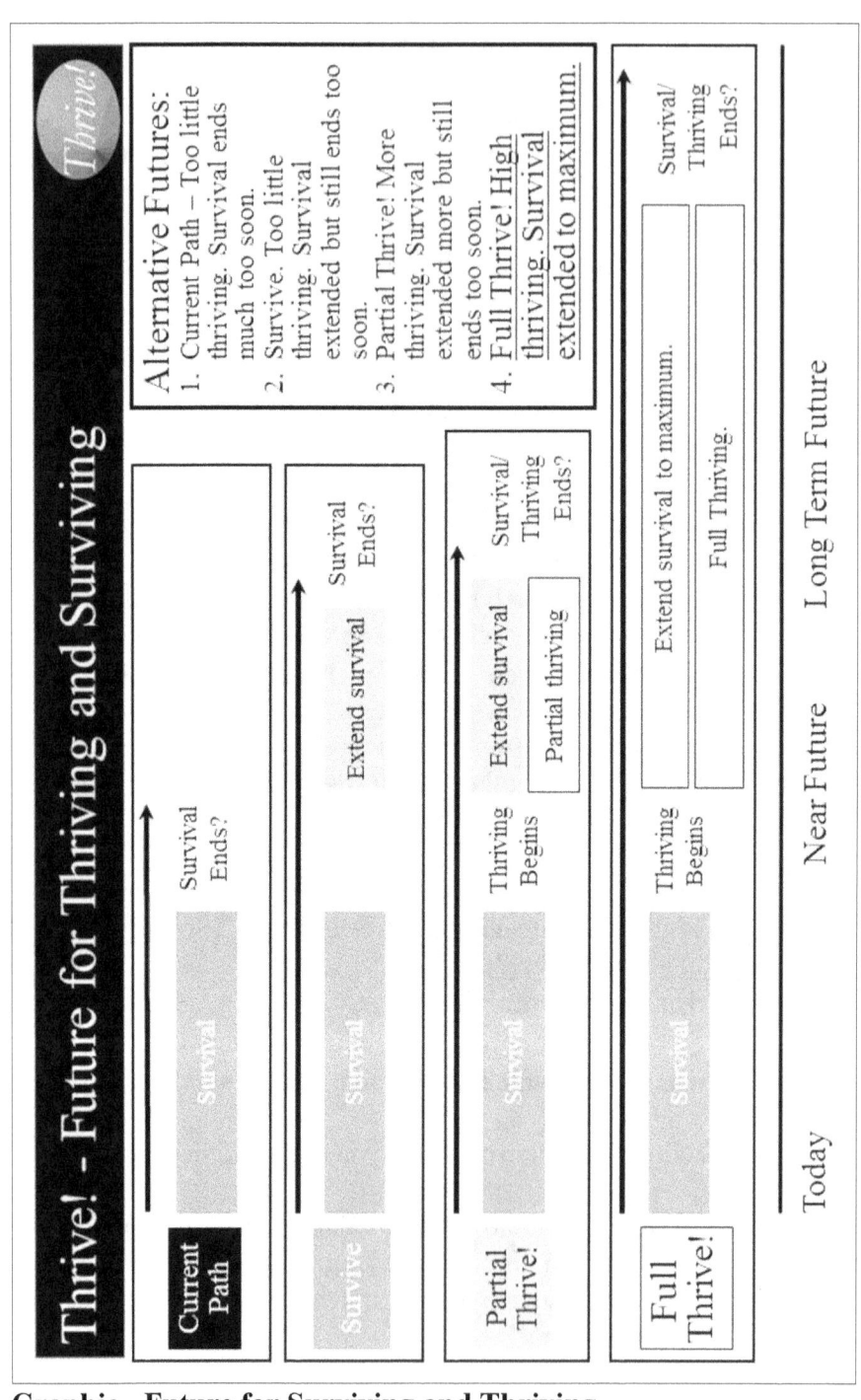

Graphic - Future for Surviving and Thriving

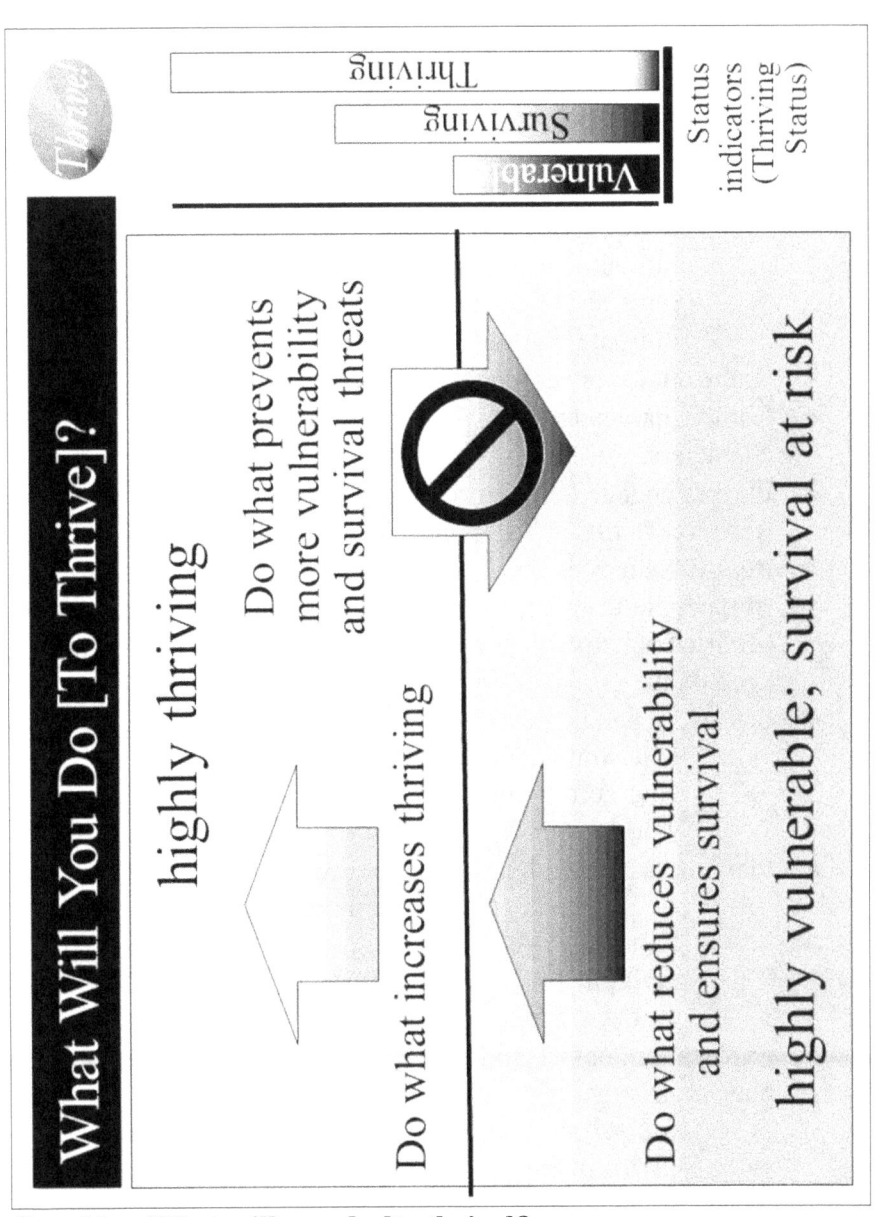

Graphic - What will you do [to thrive]?

This is "Thrive!".

- "Game" choice is:
    - single-player (you for yourself),
    - multiplayer (you and your community for your community; choose whether friends, family, affinity group, local community, state, country, or region), or
    - ultimate massively multiplayer is Thrive Endeavor (you and all of us now and future) for the world+ with ultimate win of "all thrive forever".
- Game choice is simulation or real-life mode.
- Game Characters. You. Simulation and/or real-life characters.
- Players engage together on strategy, tactics, logistics (resources), obstacles, internal/external changes, and action.
- Real-life enemies make or keep people vulnerable and/or stop people from surviving and thriving. Change them. Real-life friends help you survive and thrive. Get, support and keep them
- Setting, depending on the game choice is:
    - your immediate environment,
    - your community, or
    - world+ (our world and beyond).
- Play map is drawn by players for the play environment:
    - single-player (your immediate environment now and future),
    - multiplayer (your community now and future), and
    - ultimate massively multiplayer (world+ forever).
- Exploration, before and during play, is of your ever-changing play environment:
    - yourself and your immediate internal/external environment,
    - yourself and your community and its internal/external environment,
    - yourself and the world+ and its environment.
- Play is real-time - now, near and far future, and forever.
- "Wins and losses" are for near and far future. Ultimate win is for forever. Wins and losses are real.

Play Thrive! in real life in real-time with real people with real consequences.

0. How to "play" "Thrive! – All Thrive Forever". How to survive and thrive.
1. What will you do so you thrive?
    - Single Player, Real-time
    - Win – you survive and thrive near future and far future.
2. What will you and your community do so it thrives?
    - Multiplayer, Real-time
    - Win – you and your community survive and thrive near future and far future.
3. What will Thrive Endeavor (you and all of us now and future) do for world+ so all thrive forever?
    - Ultimate Massively Multiplayer, Real-time, Late Game
    - Ultimate win - "all thrive forever"

Time to play. Go to "How to play". Or go immediately to your choice of "game" (you, your community, or world+).

[Web version @ ThriveForever.org]

How to Play. How to Survive and Thrive.

Game. Choose your "game":
- Single-player (you for yourself),
- Multiplayer (you and your community for your community), or
- Ultimate massively multiplayer is Thrive Endeavor (you and all of us now and future) with ultimate win of "all thrive forever".

Mode. Choose simulation or real-life.

Game Characters. You. Simulation and/or real-life characters.

Players. Choose (if multiplayer) other players (non-enemy) and their role, motivation and ability. Specific abilities and motivation lead to greater success in specific roles. Choose the team well. Play as a team. Best if whole team (before and during play) helps make choices ("play", future, path, location, time), draw play map, identify enemies and friends, and explore. Good communication is very important.

"Enemies and Friends". Identify real-life friends who help you win. They may or may not be on your team. Identify real-life enemies who make or keep people vulnerable and/or stop people from surviving and thriving. They are defeated when there remain no threats to surviving and thriving.

Path and Future. Choose path (Survive, Partial Thrive, and Full Thrive) you will take and future (Survive, Partial Thrive, and Full Thrive) you will seek. Get off Current Path to avoid losing.

Win. Choose "win". Reduce vulnerability. Survive and thrive today, near future, far future. Ultimate win in ultimate massively multiplayer game is "all thrive forever" (you and all of us survive and thrive today, near and far future, and forever). [Use Scoresheet. Win? How well and for how long?] Download fillable scoresheet via ThriveForever.org

Play Location. Choose location best for play and achieving best future. Virtual location (online play). Physical location. Combination is best.

Play Time. Choose start time. Play real-time with pauses at least for strategy and rest.

Environment/Setting. Identify environment for chosen game.
- your immediate environment,
- your community, or
- world+ (our world and beyond).

Pay attention and adjust to changing environment.

Map. Draw map for game's play environment.
- single-player (your immediate environment now and future),
- multiplayer (your community (which can be friends, family, affinity group, local community, state, country or region) now and future), or
- ultimate massively multiplayer (world+ forever).

Exploration. Explore, before and during play, your game's ever-changing play environment.
- yourself and your immediate internal/external environment,
- yourself and your community and its internal/external environment, or
- yourself and the world+ and its environment.

Information gathering helps with strategy, tactics and actions.

Resources. Identify resources to be used during play. Includes people, things, money that help win.

Obstacles. Identify obstacles to overcome. These change.

Strategy and Tactics. Choose initial strategy and tactics and how they will be adjusted during play.

Play. Play real-time - now, near and far future, and forever. Adjust above elements as needed during play.

1. Play! Win near and far future!
2. Execute strategy and tactics.
    - Use Overall Thrive! strategy and action plan
3. Act. Winning?
    - Use Worksheet - Thrive! Strategy & Action Plan. What actions taken? Who did what to/with whom, where, when? With what result?
    - Use Thrive Scoresheet - Win? How well are you and for how long? As alternative, you may want to use Thrive (Excel) Scoresheet - Win? How well and for how long? to enter previous information and calculate score. Download fillable scoresheet via ThriveForever.org
4. If winning, congratulations! If losing, do better!
5. Adjust strategies, tactics and actions during play.
6. Pause. Rest?
7. Play! Win!
8. Win or lose, continue "game". This is real life.
9. Play!
10. Win surviving and thriving future. **Ultimate score is 150,000!**
    - See Graphic - Thrive Score: Winning? Thriving?

Want the ultimate challenge? Up your "game" to play and win ultimate massively multiplayer world+ and help win "all thrive forever"? Go to Game 3.

Worksheet - *Thrive!* Strategy & Action Plan. What actions taken?

Thriving and Surviving	Actions - Who did what to/with whom, where, when, and with what result?
Performing (live/ work/play) well?	
Well-off?	
Well nourished?	
Well housed?	
Well protected?	
Well educated?	
Physically/ mentally well?	
Growing/ developing well?	
Living in good habitat?	
Not vulnerable?	
Producing personal/public goods?	
Stable, positive climate?	
Sustainable?	

Thrive Scoresheet - Win? How well and for how long?

* **You or Community:** Near – < 5 years. Far – 5-25 years. Forever – > 25 years.
  World+: Near – < 5 years. Far – 5-100 years. Forever – > 100 years.

Thriving and Surviving	How well? Not survive? Survive? Thrive? [Pick one] _0 NotS 50 Survive 100 Thrive	How long? * Near future? Far future? Forever? [Pick one] _25 Near 75 Far 100 Forever	Score [How well x How long]
Performing (live/work/play) well?			
Well-off?			
Well nourished?			
Well housed?			
Well protected?			
Well educated?			
Physically/mentally well?			
Growing/developing well?			
Living in good habitat?			
Not vulnerable?			
Producing personal/public goods?			
Stable, positive climate?			
Sustainable?			
		Bonus – if 10,000 on all, add 20,000	
		Total Win Ultimate - 150,000	

Thrive (Excel) Scoresheet - Win? How well and for how long?

Download fillable scoresheet via ThriveForever.org

Graphic - Thrive Score: Winning? Thriving?

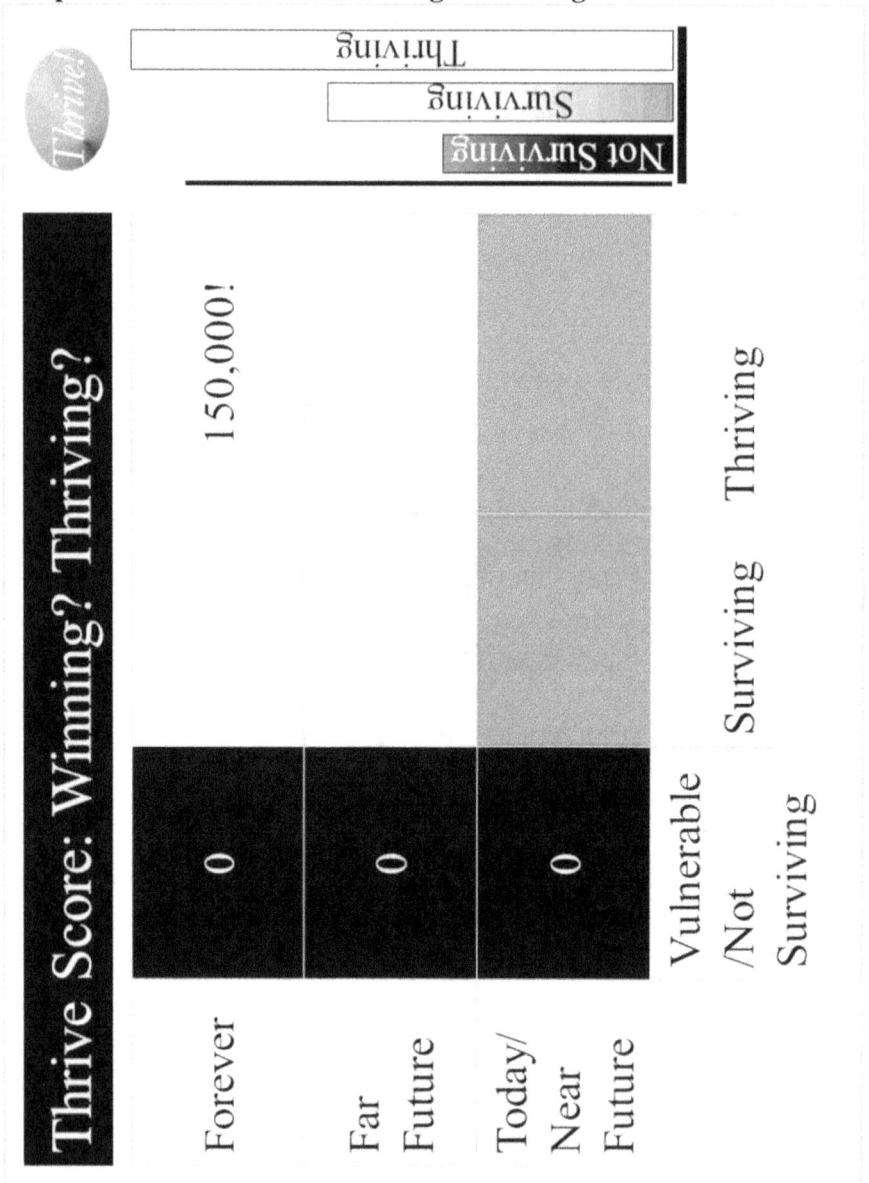

- 14 -

1: "Game" 1: What Will <u>You</u> Do So <u>You</u> Thrive?
[Single Player]

[TOC]

- "Play" – You for your future. Single player. Real-life. Real-time. Real people. Real consequences - a surviving and thriving future for you.
- Win – You survive and thrive near future, far future.
- Setting - Your immediate environment

[Web version @ ThriveForever.org]

Context.

Why you <u>can</u> win.

In this "game" and real life, you <u>can</u> win and have a surviving and thriving future. To "win" that future, keep in mind that you are different with a different future already beginning. Whether that future appears bad or good, you can do better. To build a better future, use Thrive strategy, tactics and actions that have been used successfully at the personal level and on larger scales (community, country). [3] They can work for you. As they have for others, this strategy can help you win by building, achieving and sustaining a surviving and thriving future.

Why you <u>must</u> win.

---

[3] To win and build a surviving and thriving future for you and your community, Thrive can be helpful to you. The **Thrive! Next Generation Toolkit** is laid out in the full **People's Guide** and in ***Thrive! - Building a Thriving Future*** - a manual providing greater depth on strategy and tools and available via Amazon.com or free download from ThrivingFuture.org.

You must win and have a surviving and thriving future. You must do better whether your future appears bad or good. Why? Even those people that have a good future are not fully thriving, are not likely to be fully thriving in the future, and are still facing uncertainties about the long term future. You want and need a surviving and thriving future because your future is endangered and because of our human need to survive and desire to thrive. What drives a person is our human need to survive and desire to thrive now and in a sustainable future. Further, because people (past and present) have broken some part of your world and endangered its future, you and others (present and future) must help fix what is broken and build a survivable and thriving future.

Key to winning the "game" is the strong desire by you to move from your current vulnerabilities through and beyond surviving to a sustained thriving future.

Getting Started.

[TOC]

Getting started with Thrive! – All Thrive Forever "game". [4] **Single player. Real-life. Real-time. Real people. Real consequences - a surviving and thriving future for you**.

1. **Game.** Single player (you for yourself).
2. **Mode.** Choose simulation or real-life.
3. **Players.** You alone, though you may get help. What is your ability, motivation and expected behavior? Specific abilities and motivation lead to greater success.
4. **Game Characters.** You. Simulation and/or real-life characters.
5. **Single Play.** Play as individual.
6. **Win.** Choose win. Reduce vulnerability. Survive and thrive today, near future, far future. [Use Scoresheet - Win? How well are you and for how long?] Download fillable scoresheet via ThriveForever.org
7. **Path and Future.** Choose path (Survive, Partial Thrive, and Full Thrive) you will take and future (Survive, Partial Thrive, and Full Thrive) you will seek. Get off Current Path to avoid losing. [See Graphic - Future for Person's Thriving and Surviving]
8. **Play Location.** Choose location best for play and achieving best future.
9. **Play Time.** Choose start time. Play real-time with pauses at least for strategy and rest.
10. **"Enemies and Friends".** Identify real-life friends who help you win. For each, what is ability, motivation and expected behavior? For friends, determine what positive actions each is or will take and why. Identify real-life enemies who make or keep people vulnerable and/or stop people from surviving and thriving. For each, what is ability, motivation and expected behavior? For enemies, determine what negative actions each is or will take and why. They are defeated when there remain no threats to surviving and thriving.
11. **Environment/Setting.** Your world and its surrounding environment. Pay attention and adjust to changing environment.

---

[4] Free download of larger, fillable scoresheet via ThriveForever.org

12. **Map.** Draw map for play environment. Your world
13. **Exploration.** Explore, before and during play, your ever-changing play environment – your world and its internal/external environment. Information gathering helps with strategy, tactics and actions.
14. **Resources.** Identify resources to be used during play. Includes people, things, money that help win.
15. **Obstacles.** Identify obstacles to overcome. These change.
16. **Strategy, Tactics and Actions (Starting).** Having chosen the path (Survive, Partial Thrive, and Full Thrive) you will take and the future (Survive, Partial Thrive, and Full Thrive) you will seek, strategize on how to get off Current Path to avoid losing and get on chosen path to chosen future and win. Strategize. First, near future. Second, far future. Third, forever. Or do simultaneous push for all three.
    - How well (surviving/ thriving) should your world be in the future?
    - What has to change to achieve your thriving future?
    - What actions by you are needed to achieve your thriving future?
    - Overall Thrive! strategy and action plan
17. **Adjust above elements as needed during play.**

Play.

[TOC]

Play Thrive! – All Thrive Forever "game" and win surviving and thriving future for you.

1. **Play!** Win near and far future!
2. Execute strategy and tactics.
   - Use Overall Thrive! strategy and action plan
3. Act. Winning?
   - Use Worksheet - Thrive! Strategy and Action Plan. What actions taken? Who did what to/with whom, where, when? With what result?
   - Use Thrive Scoresheet - Win? How well are you and for how long? As alternative, you may want to use Thrive (Excel) Scoresheet to enter previous information and calculate score. Download fillable scoresheet via ThriveForever.org
4. If winning, congratulations! If losing, do better!
5. Adjust strategies, tactics and actions during play.
6. Pause. Rest?
7. Play! Win!
8. **Win or lose, continue "game".** This is real life.
9. **Play!** Win surviving and thriving future. **Ultimate score is 150,000!**
   - See Graphic - Thrive Score: Winning? Thriving?

Want the ultimate challenge? Up your "game" to play and win ultimate massively multiplayer world+ and help win "all thrive forever"? Go to Game 3.

Path and Future. *[Back]*

During "play", you and all of us face four possible futures [See Graphic - Future for Person's Thriving and Surviving]:

- Current Path where there is little thriving and survival ends much too soon. Loss.
- Survive Path where there is little thriving and survival is extended but still ends too soon. Smaller loss.
- Partial Thrive Path where there is more thriving and survival is extended more but still ends too soon. Partial win.
- Full Thrive Path where there is high thriving and survival is extended to maximum. Ultimate win.

To avoid losing, get off Current Path. For ultimate win, get on Full Thrive Path where you and all of us survive and thrive today, near and far future, and forever.

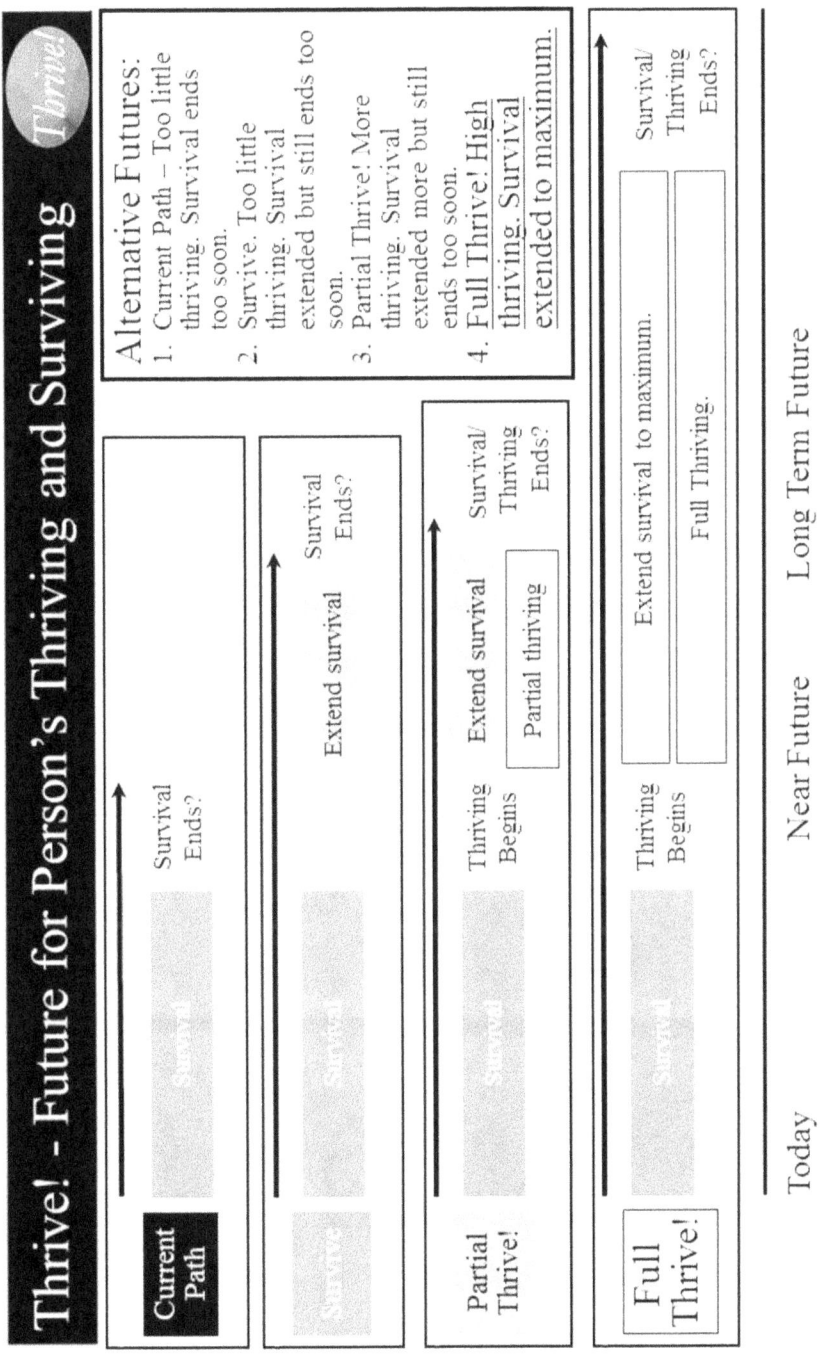

Graphic - Future for Person's Thriving and Surviving

How well (surviving/ thriving) should you be in the future?
[Back]

What should your world be in the future? How well should you as a whole be in the future? Overall, you should be <u>surviving and thriving</u>. With this as a guide, you choose the surviving and thriving future you want to build and achieve.

Use <u>Worksheet - What should your world be and how well?</u> to describe the desired future with respect to performing well? Being well-off (financially). Being well nourished (food and drink)? Being well housed? Being well protected (exposures, crime)? Being well educated? Being physically and mentally well? Personally growing/developing well? Living within good habitat? Not being vulnerable? Producing personal and public goods? Living within a stable, positive climate? Being sustained? For each, indicate how well. Again, you should be surviving and thriving.

Thriving and Surviving	What should your world be and how well (not surviving, surviving, thriving) in the future?
Performing (live/work/play) well?	
Well-off?	
Well nourished?	
Well housed?	
Well protected?	
Well educated?	
Physically/ mentally well?	
Growing/ developing well?	
Living in good habitat?	
Not vulnerable?	
Producing personal/ public goods?	
Stable, positive climate?	
Sustainable?	

Worksheet - What should your world be and how well?

What has to change externally and internally to achieve your thriving future? *[Back]*

What has to change externally (outside of you) and internally (within you) to progress from your current status to achieve your desired surviving and thriving status? You identified what positively and negatively impacts or is likely to impact you. Update those, including any changes to your future world.

Given those, what has to change to achieve a surviving and thriving future? Use <u>Worksheet - Thrive! Strategy & Action Plan. What changes needed?</u> to describe all that has to change externally and internally.

Good changes improve and/or sustain surviving and thriving. Bad changes prevent and/or limit surviving and thriving.

Thriving and Surviving	Changes needed to achieve surviving and thriving future
Performing (live/ work/play) well?	
Well-off?	
Well nourished?	
Well housed?	
Well protected?	
Well educated?	
Physically/ mentally well?	
Growing/ developing well?	
Living in good habitat?	
Not vulnerable?	
Producing personal/public goods?	
Stable, positive climate?	
Sustainable?	

Worksheet - *Thrive!* **Strategy & Action Plan. What changes needed?**

What actions by you are needed to achieve your thriving future? *[Back]*

What internal actions (by you) and external actions (by others) are needed to bring about needed changes that improve your world to achieve surviving and thriving status? [See Graphic - What will you do so you thrive?]

External actions by others. Very important external actions are needed. What external actions by others will bring about needed changes? Use Worksheet - Thrive! Strategy & Action Plan. What actions needed?

Identify external actions by others that support good changes that will help improve and/or sustain surviving and thriving. If good changes are likely to occur, together with others support them. If good changes are not likely to occur, together with others support them and develop other good changes to compensate.

Identify external actions by others that stop bad changes that prevent or limit surviving and thriving. If bad changes are not likely to occur, together with others ensure they do not. If bad changes are likely to occur, together with others change them, stop them or avoid/reduce their impact.

Internal actions by you. Very important internal actions are needed. Use Worksheet - Thrive! Strategy & Action Plan. What actions needed?

Identify internal actions by you that support good changes that will help improve and/or sustain surviving and thriving. If good changes are likely to occur, support them. If good changes are not likely to occur, support them and develop other good changes to compensate.

Identify internal actions by you that stop bad changes that prevent or limit surviving and thriving. If bad changes are not likely to occur, ensure they do not. If bad changes are likely to occur, change them, stop them or avoid/reduce their impact.

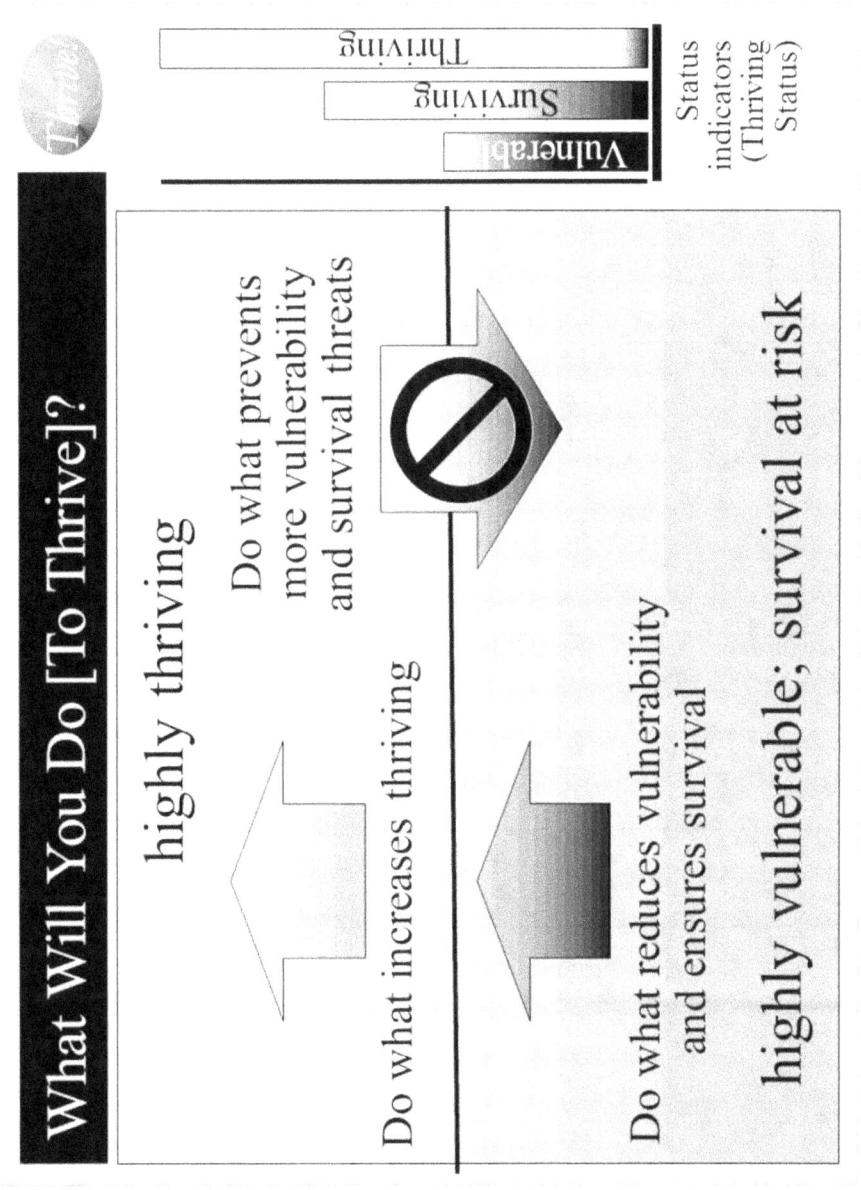

Graphic - What will you do so you thrive?

Thriving and Surviving	Actions - Who will do what to/with whom, where, when, and with what result?
Performing (live/ work/play) well?	
Well-off?	
Well nourished?	
Well housed?	
Well protected?	
Well educated?	
Physically/ mentally well?	
Growing/ developing well?	
Living in good habitat?	
Not vulnerable?	
Producing personal/public goods?	
Stable, positive climate?	
Sustainable?	

Worksheet - *Thrive!* Strategy & Action Plan. What actions needed?

Overall Thrive! strategy, tactics and actions. *[Back]*

Your overall *Thrive!* strategy, tactics and actions will be your *Thrive!* **Strategy and Action Plan**. [5] For each action, designate who (you and others) will do what to/with whom, where, when, with what resources and with what result. Use <u>Worksheet - Actions: Who, what, whom, when, where, resources, result</u> to document detailed actions and responsibilities. Make sure you have all actions needed to build, achieve and sustain your surviving and thriving.

As the strategy is executed, your strategy, actions and results should be updated in your *Thrive!* **Strategy and Action Plan**.

Periodically, you should assess your strategies/actions near and long term impact on near and long term surviving and thriving. When a) your strategies and actions are not building and sustaining a thriving future and/or b) there are changes in your world, adjust your *Thrive!* **Strategy and Action Plan**.

Successfully execute your *Thrive!* **Strategy and Action Plan** to build a near and long term surviving and thriving future. You (and any others) must successfully carry out the assigned action and do what is required to/with whoever is required, where required, when required, and with what needed/desired result. A *Thrive!* **Strategy and Action Plan** is only as good as its successful execution and successful achievement of the desired outcome - a surviving and thriving future. *[Following is an example of **Thrive! Strategy and Action Plan** for your surviving <u>and</u> thriving future.]*

---

[5] To win and build a surviving and thriving future for you, Thrive can be helpful to you. The **Thrive! Next Generation Toolkit** is laid out in the full **People's Guide** and in *Thrive! - Building a Thriving Future* - a manual providing greater depth on strategy and tools and available via Amazon.com or free download from ThrivingFuture.org.

Who	Does What	To/With Whom	When	Where	With What Resources	With What Result

Worksheet - Actions: Who, what, whom, when, where, resources, result.

Example of your surviving and thriving. *To build, achieve and sustain your surviving and thriving future, the* **Thrive! Strategy and Action Plan** *should be more like the following example: [Who will do what to/with whom, where, when, and with what result?]*

Starting immediately, you build, achieve, and sustain a surviving and thriving future, including:
- Performing well. *Starting immediately, you act to ensure a) you can work and earn a living income sufficient to survive and thrive and b) you have sufficient resources for and are living, recreating, learning so that you are surviving and thriving to maximum extent feasible.*
- Being well-off (financially). *Starting immediately, you act to ensure you have sufficient income/resources to survive and thrive.*
- Being well nourished (food and drink). *Starting immediately, you act to ensure, that you have access to, be able to afford and consume healthy foods enough to survive and thrive.*
- Being well housed. *Starting immediately, you act to ensure you have access to, be able to afford and live in adequate and preferably high performing housing that supports surviving and thriving.*
- Being well protected (exposures, crime). *Starting immediately, you act to ensure environmental exposures in home, workplace and elsewhere are minimized so as to not prevent surviving and thriving.*
- Being well educated. *Starting immediately, you act to ensure you are educated to the full extent of your abilities, needs and desires and to support their surviving and thriving.*
- Being physically and mentally well. *Starting immediately, you act to ensure a) you receive the optimal health support to ensure, within the next 20 years, surviving and thriving and b) physical and mental health is optimized to best ensure surviving and thriving.*
- Personally growing/developing well. *Starting immediately, you act to ensure you are personally growing and developing to best ensure surviving and thriving.*
- Living within good habitat. *Starting immediately, you act to ensure a) you have access to habitat that best supports their surviving and thriving.*

- Not being vulnerable. *Starting immediately, you act to ensure you, if vulnerable, are vulnerable only to the minimum extent feasible.*
- Producing personal and public goods. *Starting immediately, you act to ensure you produce personal and public goods (including personal income/resources, housing, food and drink, energy, education, health, protection, personal growth and development, and habitat) so as to support surviving and thriving.*
- Living within a stable, positive climate. *Starting immediately, you act to ensure you behave so as to avoid negative impacts and support positive impacts so as to help ensure a stable, positive climate.*
- Being sustained. *Starting immediately, you act to ensure you behave so as to ensure your sustainability.*

Worksheet - Thrive! Strategy & Action Plan. What actions taken?

Thriving and Surviving	Actions - Who did what to/with whom, where, when, and with what result?
Performing (live/ work/play) well?	
Well-off?	
Well nourished?	
Well housed?	
Well protected?	
Well educated?	
Physically/ mentally well?	
Growing/ developing well?	
Living in good habitat?	
Not vulnerable?	
Producing personal/public goods?	
Stable, positive climate?	
Sustainable?	

Thrive Scoresheet - Win? How well are you and for how long?

* Near – less than 5 years. Far – 5-25 years. Forever – more than 10 years.

Thriving and Surviving	How well? Not survive? Survive? Thrive? [Pick one] 0 NotS 50 Survive 100 Thrive	How long? * Near future? Far future? Forever? [Pick one] 25 Near 75 Far 100 Forever	Score [How well x How long]
Performing (live/work/play) well?			
Well-off?			
Well nourished?			
Well housed?			
Well protected?			
Well educated?			
Physically/mentally well?			
Growing/developing well?			
Living in good habitat?			
Not vulnerable?			
Producing personal /public goods?			
Stable, positive climate?			
Sustainable?			
		Bonus – if 10,000 on all, add 20,000	
		Total Win Ultimate - 150,000	

Thrive (Excel) Scoresheet - Win? How well and for how long?

Download fillable scoresheet via ThriveForever.org

Graphic - Thrive Score: Winning? Thriving?

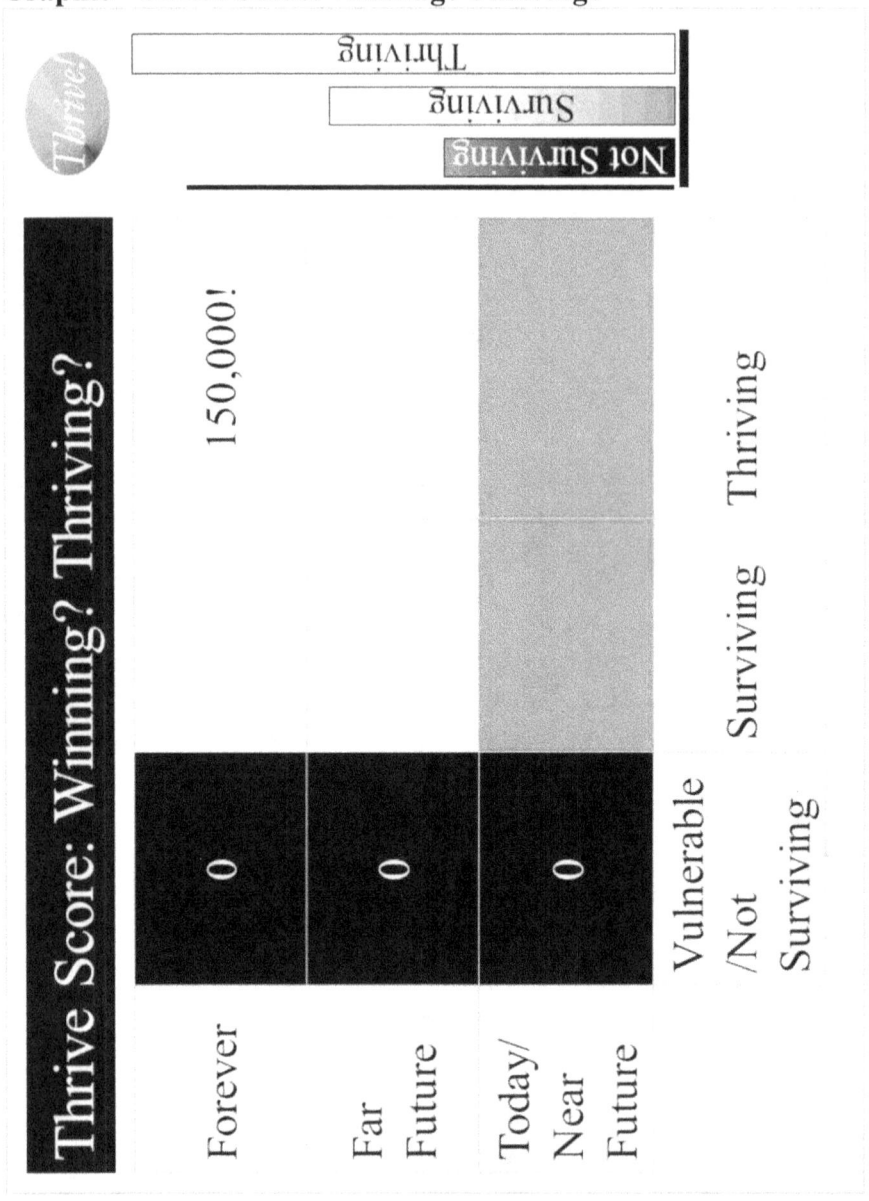

2: "Game" 2: What Will <u>You And Your Community</u> Do So It Thrives? [Play Together; Multiplayer]

[TOC]

- "Play" - You and your community for your community's future. Multiplayer. Real-life. Real-time. Real people. Real consequences - a surviving and thriving future for you and your community.
- Win – You and your community survive and thrive today, near future, far future.
- Setting - Your community

[Web version @ ThriveForever.org]

Context.

Why you and your community <u>can</u> win.

In this "game" and real life, you and your community <u>can</u> win and have a surviving and thriving future. To "win" that future, keep in mind that your community is different with a different future already beginning. Whether that future appears bad or good, your community can do better. To build a better future, use Thrive strategy, tactics and actions that have been used successfully at the personal level and on larger scales (community, country). [6] They can work for you and the community you care about. As they have for

---

[6] To win and build a surviving and thriving future for you and your community, Thrive can be helpful to you. The **Thrive! Next Generation Toolkit** is laid out in the full **People's Guide** and in ***Thrive! - Building a Thriving Future*** - a manual providing greater depth on strategy and tools and available via Amazon.com or free download from ThrivingFuture.org.

others, this strategy can help you and your community win by building, achieving and sustaining a surviving and thriving future.

Why you and your community <u>must</u> win.

You and your community <u>must</u> win and have a surviving and thriving future. Your community <u>must</u> do better whether that future appears bad or good. Why? Even if your community has a good future, your community is not fully thriving, not likely to be fully thriving in the future, and still faces uncertainties about the long term future. You and your community want and need a surviving and thriving future because your community's future is endangered and because of our human need to survive and desire to thrive. What drives your community and its people is our human need to survive and desire to thrive now and in a sustainable future. Further, because your community's people (past and present) have broken some part of your community and endangered its future, you and your community's people (present and future) must help fix what is broken and build a survivable and thriving future for your community.

Why you and your community must and can win together.

To "win" and build this better future, your community's people and leaders should be a team in this endeavor from the beginning and through each step. Winning depends on teamwork by and positive and effective leadership from your community's leaders and people. Winning depends on a collaborative, team approach where the traditional leaders and the people (also serving as leaders) jointly provide leadership, vision, motivation, strategy and successful execution. A strong team has the greater potential to "win" and create <u>and</u> sustain large, positive change and a surviving and thriving community.

Key to winning the "game" is the strong desire by you and your community to move your community from its current vulnerabilities through and beyond surviving to a sustained thriving future.

Getting Started.

[TOC]

Getting started with Thrive! – All Thrive Forever "game". [7] **Multiplayer. Real-life. Real-time. Real people. Real consequences - a surviving and thriving future for you and your community**.

1. **Game.** Multiplayer (you and your community for your community). Choose community - friends, family, affinity group, local community, state, country, or region.
2. **Mode.** Choose simulation or real-life.
3. **Players.** Choose the team well. Choose other players (non-enemy) and their role, motivation and ability. For each, what is ability, motivation and expected behavior? Specific abilities and motivation lead to greater success in specific roles. Organize team. Make iniitial decision on roles – who will do what when with what resources to produce what result. Make initial decision on how team will play as team (decisions, communication, joint and individual actions).
4. **Game Characters.** You. Simulation and/or real-life characters.
5. **Team Play.** Play as a team. Best if whole team (before and during play) helps make choices ("play", future, path, location, time), draw play map, identify enemies and friends, and explore. Good communication is very important.
6. **Win.** Choose win. Reduce vulnerability. Survive and thrive today, near future, far future. [Use Scoresheet. Win? How well is your community and for how long?] Download fillable scoresheet via ThriveForever.org
7. **Path and Future.** Choose path (Survive, Partial Thrive, and Full Thrive) you will take and future (Survive, Partial Thrive, and Full Thrive) you will seek. Get off Current Path to avoid losing. [See Graphic - Future for Community's Thriving and Surviving]
8. **Play Location.** Choose location best for play and achieving best future. Virtual location (online play). Physical location. Combination is best.
9. **Play Time.** Choose start time. Play real-time with pauses at least for strategy and rest.

---

[7] Free download of larger, fillable scoresheet via ThriveForever.org

10. **"Enemies and Friends".** Identify real-life friends who help you win. For each, what is ability, motivation and expected behavior? For friends, determine what positive actions each is or will take and why. They may or may not be on your team. Identify real-life enemies who make or keep people vulnerable and/or stop people from surviving and thriving. For each, what is ability, motivation and expected behavior? For enemies, determine what negative actions each is or will take and why. They are defeated when there remain no threats to surviving and thriving.
11. **Environment/Setting.** Your community and its surrounding environment. Pay attention and adjust to changing environment.
12. **Map.** Draw map for play environment. Your community.
13. **Exploration.** Explore, before and during play, your ever-changing play environment - yourself and your community and its internal/external environment. Information gathering helps with strategy, tactics and actions.
14. **Resources.** Identify resources to be used during play. Includes people, things, money that help win.
15. **Obstacles.** Identify obstacles to overcome. These change.
16. **Strategy, Tactics and Actions (Starting).** Having chosen the path (Survive, Partial Thrive, and Full Thrive) you will take and the future (Survive, Partial Thrive, and Full Thrive) you will seek, strategize on how to get off Current Path to avoid losing and get on chosen path to chosen future and win. Strategize. First, near future. Second, far future. Third, forever. Or do simultaneous push for all three.
    - How well should your community be in the future?
    - What has to change to achieve your community's thriving future?
    - What actions by your community are needed to achieve its thriving future?
    - Overall Thrive! strategy and action plan
17. **Adjust above elements as needed during play.**

Play.

[TOC]

Play <u>Thrive! – All Thrive Forever</u> "game" and win surviving and thriving future for you and your community.

1. **Play!** Win near and far future!
2. Execute strategy and tactics.
   - Use Overall Thrive! strategy and action plan
3. Act. Winning?
   - Use Worksheet - Thrive! Strategy and Action Plan. What actions taken? Who did what to/with whom, where, when? With what result?
   - Use Thrive Scoresheet - Win? How well is your community and for how long? As alternative, you may want to use Thrive (Excel) Scoresheet - Win? How well and for how long? to enter previous information and calculate score. Download fillable scoresheet via ThriveForever.org
4. If winning, congratulations! If losing, do better!
5. Adjust strategies, tactics and actions during play.
6. Pause. Rest?
7. Play! Win!
8. **Win or lose, continue "game".** This is real life.
9. **Play!** Win surviving and thriving future. **Ultimate score is 150,000!**
   - See Graphic - Thrive Score: Winning? Thriving?

Want the ultimate challenge? Up your "game" to play and win ultimate massively multiplayer world+ and help win "all thrive forever"? Go to Game 3.

5. Path and Future. *[Back]*

During "play", you and all of us face four possible futures [See Graphic - Future for Community's Thriving and Surviving]:

- Current Path where there is little thriving and survival ends much too soon. Loss.
- Survive Path where there is little thriving and survival is extended but still ends too soon. Smaller loss.
- Partial Thrive Path where there is more thriving and survival is extended more but still ends too soon. Partial win.
- Full Thrive Path where there is high thriving and survival is extended to maximum. Ultimate win.

To avoid losing, get off Current Path. For ultimate win, get on Full Thrive Path where you and all of us survive and thrive today, near and far future, and forever.

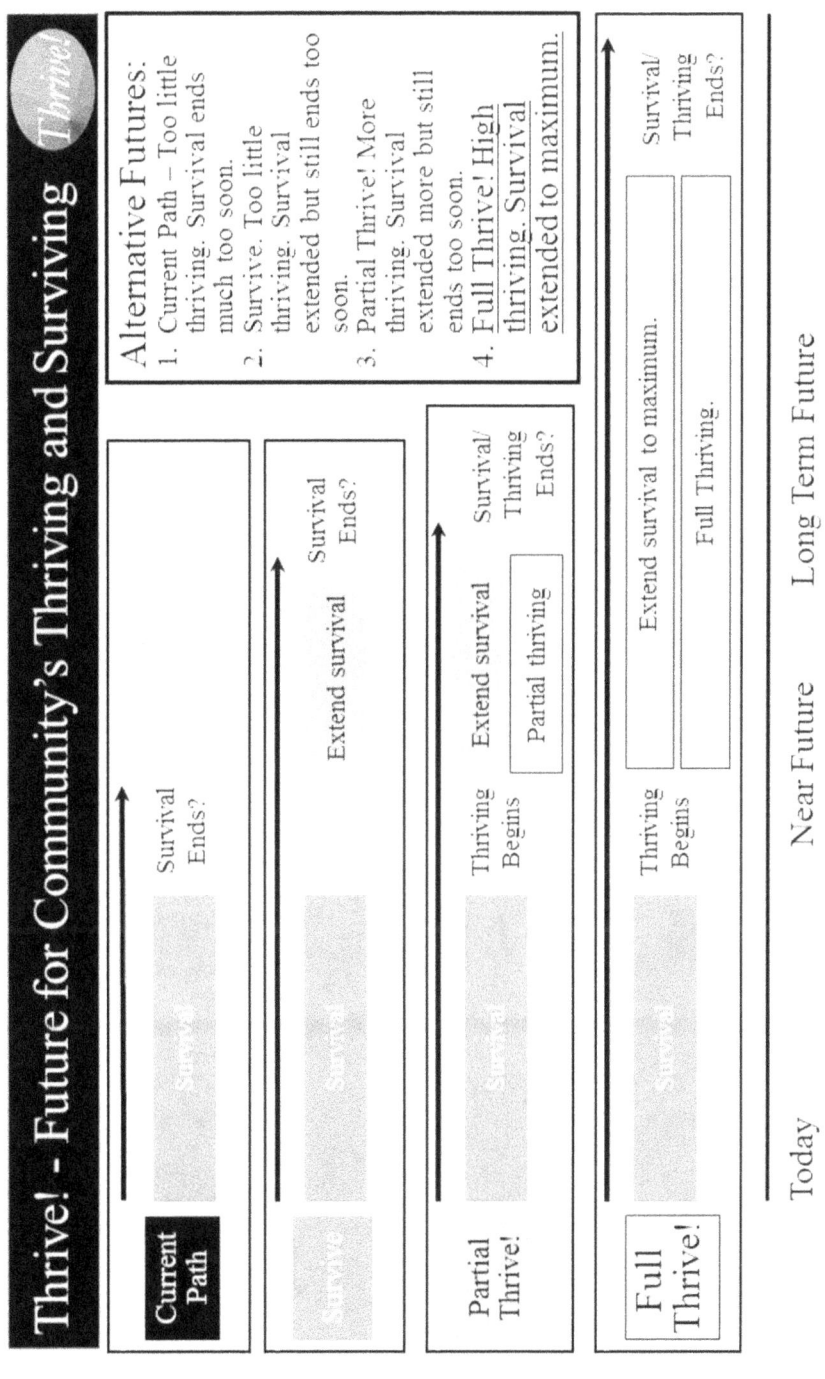

Graphic - Future for Community's Thriving and Surviving

What should your community be and how well in the future?
[Back]

What should your community be in the future? How well should your community as a whole be in the future? Overall, your community should be <u>surviving and thriving</u>. With this as a guide, you choose the surviving and thriving future your community wants to build and achieve.

Use <u>Worksheet - What should your community be and how well?</u> to describe the desired future with respect to performing well? Being well-off (financially). Being well nourished (food and drink)? Being well housed? Being well protected (exposures, crime)? Being well educated? Being physically and mentally well? Personally growing/developing well? Living within good habitat? Not being vulnerable? Producing personal and public goods? Living within a stable, positive climate? Being sustained? For each, indicate how well. Again, your community should be surviving and thriving.

Thriving and Surviving	What should your community be and how well (not surviving, surviving, thriving) in the future?
Performing (live/work/play) well?	
Well-off?	
Well nourished?	
Well housed?	
Well protected?	
Well educated?	
Physically/ mentally well?	
Growing/ developing well?	
Living in good habitat?	
Not vulnerable?	
Producing personal/ public goods?	
Stable, positive climate?	
Sustainable?	

Worksheet - What should your community be and how well?

What has to change externally and internally to achieve your community's thriving future? *[Back]*

What has to change externally (outside your community) and internally (within your community) to progress from your community's current status to achieve your desired surviving and thriving status? You identified what positively and negatively impacts or is likely to impact your community. Update those, including any changes to your future community.

Given those, what has to change to achieve a surviving and thriving future? Use <u>Worksheet - Thrive! Strategy and Action Plan. What changes needed?</u> to describe all that has to change externally and internally.

Good changes improve and/or sustain surviving and thriving. Bad changes prevent and/or limit surviving and thriving.

Thriving and Surviving	Changes needed to achieve surviving and thriving future
Performing (live/ work/play) well?	
Well-off?	
Well nourished?	
Well housed?	
Well protected?	
Well educated?	
Physically/ mentally well?	
Growing/ developing well?	
Living in good habitat?	
Not vulnerable?	
Producing personal/public goods?	
Stable, positive climate?	
Sustainable?	

Worksheet - *Thrive!* Strategy and Action Plan. What changes needed?

What actions by your community are needed to achieve its thriving future? *[Back]*

What internal actions (by you and your community) and external actions (by others) are needed to bring about needed changes that improve your community to achieve surviving and thriving status? [See Graphic - What will your community do so it thrives?]

External actions by others. Very important external actions are needed. What external actions by others will bring about needed changes? Use Worksheet - Thrive! Strategy and Action Plan. What actions needed? Identify external actions by others that support good changes that will help improve and/or sustain surviving and thriving. If good changes are likely to occur, together with others support them. If good changes are not likely to occur, together with others support them and develop other good changes to compensate.

Identify external actions by others that stop bad changes that prevent or limit surviving and thriving. If bad changes are not likely to occur, together with others ensure they do not. If bad changes are likely to occur, together with others change them, stop them or avoid/reduce their impact.

Internal actions by your community. Very important internal actions are needed. Individual community members and your community as a whole should support your strategy. Use Worksheet - Thrive! Strategy and Action Plan. What actions needed? Identify internal actions by your community that support good changes that will help improve and/or sustain surviving and thriving. If good changes are likely to occur, support them. If good changes are not likely to occur, support them and develop other good changes to compensate.

Identify internal actions by your community that stop bad changes that prevent or limit surviving and thriving. If bad changes are not likely to occur, ensure they do not. If bad changes are likely to occur, change them, stop them or avoid/reduce their impact.

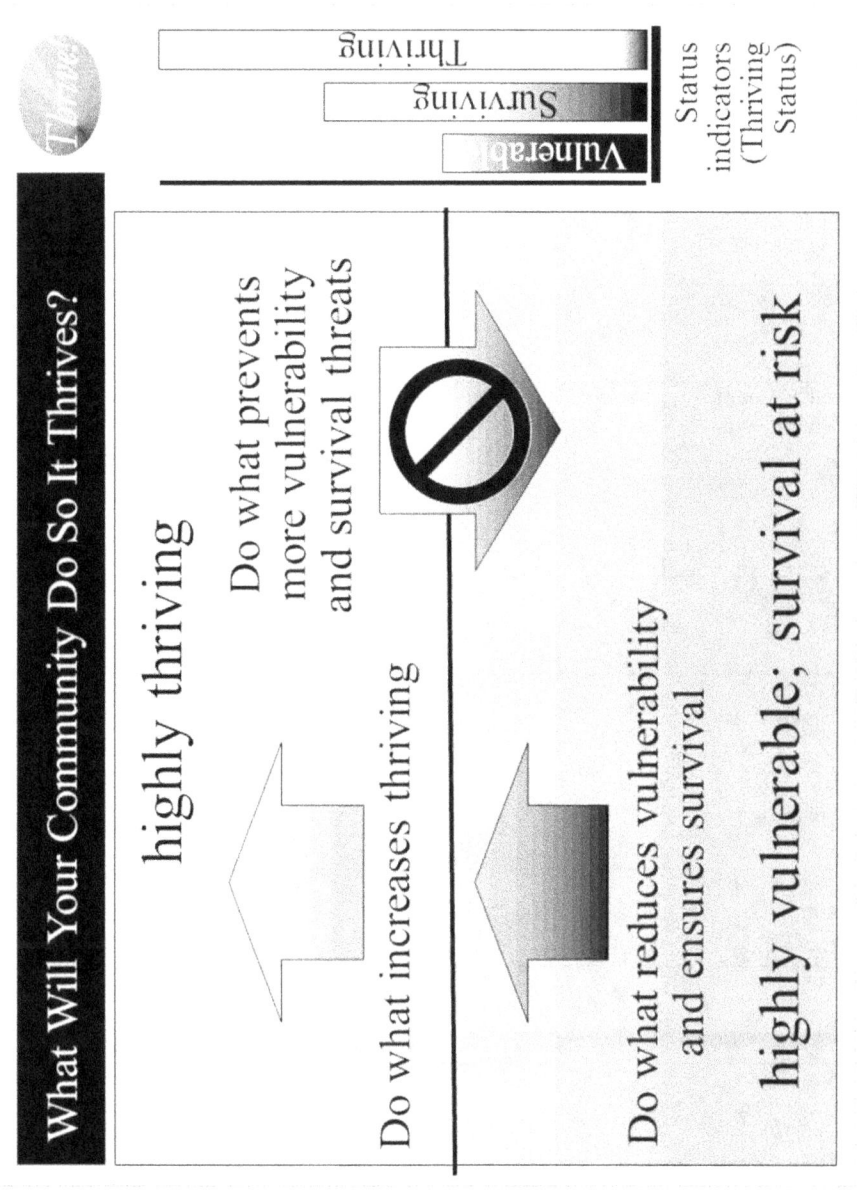

Graphic - What will your community do so it thrives?

Thriving and Surviving	Actions - Who will do what to/with whom, where, when, and with what result?
Performing (live/ work/play) well?	
Well-off?	
Well nourished?	
Well housed?	
Well protected?	
Well educated?	
Physically/ mentally well?	
Growing/ developing well?	
Living in good habitat?	
Not vulnerable?	
Producing personal/public goods?	
Stable, positive climate?	
Sustainable?	

Worksheet - *Thrive!* Strategy and Action Plan. What actions needed?

Overall *Thrive!* strategy, tactics and actions. *[Back]*

Your overall ***Thrive!*** strategy, tactics and actions need to be agreed to by your community. This will be your community's ***Thrive!*** **Strategy and Action Plan**. [8] Different members of your community will take on different responsibilities. For each action, designate who of your community will do what to/with whom, where, when, with what resources and with what result. Use <u>Worksheet - Actions: Who, what, whom, when, where, resources, result</u> to document detailed actions and responsibilities. Make sure you have all actions needed to build, achieve and sustain a surviving and thriving community.

As the strategy is executed, your strategy, actions and results should be updated in your ***Thrive!*** **Strategy and Action Plan**.

Periodically, you and your community should assess your strategies/actions near and long term impact on near and long term surviving and thriving. When a) your strategies and actions are not building and sustaining a thriving future and/or b) there are changes in the external world or in your community, adjust your ***Thrive!*** **Strategy and Action Plan**.

Successfully execute your community's ***Thrive!*** **Strategy and Action Plan** and to build a near and long term surviving and thriving future. Each and all must successfully carry out the assigned action and do what is required to/with whoever is required, where required, when required, and with what needed/desired result. A ***Thrive!*** **Strategy and Action Plan** is only as good as its successful execution and successful achievement of the desired outcome - a surviving and thriving future. *[Following is an example of **Thrive!** Strategy and Action Plan for you and your community's surviving <u>and</u> thriving future.]*

---

[8] To win and build a surviving and thriving future for you and your community, Thrive can be helpful to you. The **Thrive! Next Generation Toolkit** is laid out in the full **People's Guide** and in ***Thrive! - Building a Thriving Future*** - a manual providing greater depth on strategy and tools and available via Amazon.com or free download from ThrivingFuture.org.

Who	Does What	To/With Whom	When	Where	With What Resources	With What Result

Worksheet - Actions: Who, what, whom, when, where, resources, result.

Example of you and your community surviving __and__ thriving. To build, achieve and sustain a surviving __and__ thriving future, the **Thrive! Strategy and Action Plan** *for you and your community should be more like the following example: [Who will do what to/with whom, where, when, with what resources with what result?]*

Starting immediately for you and your community, people, business/industry, private organizations (local, country), governments (local, country) and international organizations) build, achieve, and sustain a surviving and thriving future for you and your community, including:[9]

- Performing well. *Starting immediately for you and your community, people, business/industry, private organizations (local, country), governments (local, country) and international organizations act to ensure, within the next 10 years, a) all (who are able and not appropriately retired) can work and earn a living income sufficient to survive and thrive and b) all have sufficient resources for and are living, recreating, learning so that they are surviving and thriving to maximum extent feasible.*
- Being well-off (financially). *Starting immediately for you and your community, people, business/industry, private organizations (local, country), governments (local, country) and international organizations act to ensure, within the next 10 years, a) all have sufficient income/resources to survive and thrive and b) all governments have sufficient resources to provide needed (supporting surviving) and desired (supporting thriving) public programs and policies.*
- Being well nourished (food and drink). *Starting immediately for you and your community, people, business/industry, private organizations (local, country), governments (local, country) and international organizations act to ensure, within the next 10 years, that all have access to, be able to afford and consume healthy foods enough to survive and thrive.*
- Being well housed. *Starting immediately for you and your community, people, business/industry, private organizations (local,*

---

[9] International organizations could be a major resource, especially if the community extends beyond a single country's boundaries.

country), governments (local, country) and international organizations act to ensure, within the next 20 years, all have access to, be able to afford and live in adequate and preferably high performing housing that supports surviving and thriving.

- Being well protected (exposures, crime). *Starting immediately for you and your community, people, business/industry, private organizations (local, country), governments (local, country) and international organizations act to ensure, within the next 10 years, a) environmental exposures in home, workplace and elsewhere are minimized so as to not prevent surviving and thriving and b) crimes are minimized to the extent feasible in terms of frequency and impact so as to not prevent surviving and thriving.*

- Being well educated. *Starting immediately for you and your community, people, business/industry, private organizations (local, country), governments (local, country) and international organizations act to ensure, within the next 20 years, all are educated to the full extent of their abilities, needs and desires and to support their surviving and thriving.*

- Being physically and mentally well. *Starting immediately for you and your community, people, business/industry, private organizations (local, country), governments (local, country) and international organizations act to ensure, within the next 20 years, a) all receive the optimal health support to ensure, within the next 10 years, surviving and thriving and b) physical and mental health is optimized to best ensure surviving and thriving.*

- Personally growing/developing well. *Starting immediately for you and your community, people, business/industry, private organizations (local, country), governments (local, country) and international organizations act to ensure, within the next 10 years, all are personally growing and developing to best ensure surviving and thriving.*

- Living within good habitat. *Starting immediately for you and your community, people, business/industry, private organizations (local, country), governments (local, country) and international organizations act to ensure, within the next 10 years, a) all have access to habitat that best supports their surviving and thriving and b) your community has the optimal mix, quantity and quality of habitat to best support its inhabitants' surviving and thriving.*

- Not being vulnerable. *Starting immediately for you and your community, people, business/industry, private organizations (local, country), governments (local, country) and international organizations act to ensure, within the next 10 years, that all, if vulnerable, are vulnerable only to the minimum extent feasible.*

- Producing personal and public goods. *Starting immediately for you and your community, people, business/industry, private organizations (local, country), governments (local, country) and international organizations act to ensure, within the next 10 years, your community produces personal and public goods (including personal income/resources, housing, food and drink, energy, education, health, protection, personal growth and development, and habitat) so as to support surviving and thriving for all.*
- Living within a stable, positive climate. *Starting immediately for you and your community, people, business/industry, private organizations (local, country), governments (local, country) and international organizations act to ensure, within the next 10 years, all behave so as to avoid negative impacts and support positive impacts so as to help ensure a stable, positive climate.*
- Being sustained. *Starting immediately for you and your community, people, business/industry, private organizations (local, country), governments (local, country) and international organizations act to ensure, within the next 5 years, all people behave so as to ensure the sustainability of your community <u>and</u> its people.*

Worksheet - Thrive! Strategy & Action Plan. What actions taken?

Thriving and Surviving	Actions - Who did what to/with whom, where, when, and with what result?
Performing (live/ work/play) well?	
Well-off?	
Well nourished?	
Well housed?	
Well protected?	
Well educated?	
Physically/ mentally well?	
Growing/ developing well?	
Living in good habitat?	
Not vulnerable?	
Producing personal/public goods?	
Stable, positive climate?	
Sustainable?	

Thrive Scoresheet - Win? How well is community for how long?

* Near – less than 5 years. Far – 5-25 years. Forever – more than 25 years

Thriving and Surviving	How well? Not survive? Survive? Thrive? [Pick one] _0 NotS 50 Survive 100 Thrive	How long? * Near future? Far future? Forever? [Pick one] _25 Near _75 Far 100 Forever	Score [How well x How long]
Performing (live/ work/play) well?			
Well-off?			
Well nourished?			
Well housed?			
Well protected?			
Well educated?			
Physically/ mentally well?			
Growing/ developing well?			
Living in good habitat?			
Not vulnerable?			
Producing personal /public goods?			
Stable, positive climate?			
Sustainable?			
		Bonus – if 10,000 on all, add 20,000	
		Total Win Ultimate - 150,000	

Thrive (Excel) Scoresheet - Win? How well and for how long?

Download fillable scoresheet via ThriveForever.org

Graphic - Thrive Score: Winning? Thriving?

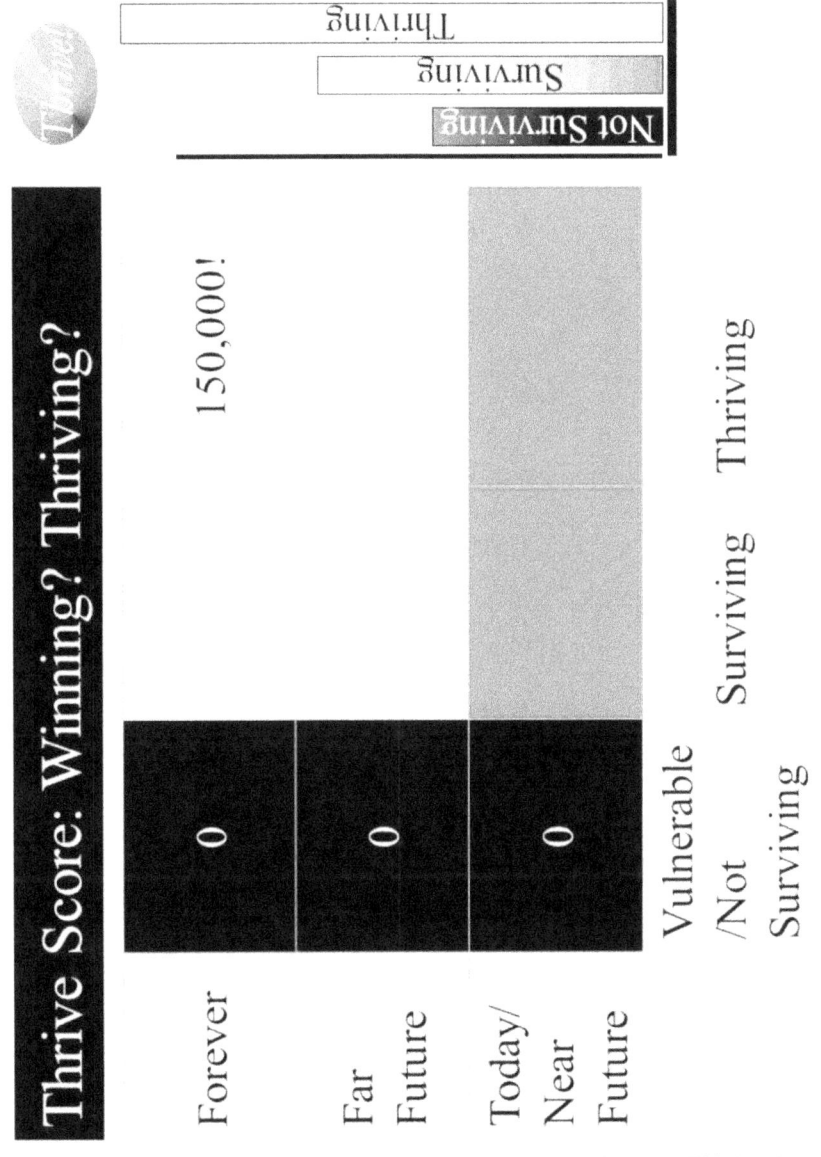

3: "Game" 3: What Will <u>Thrive! Endeavor, You and The World,</u> Do So <u>All Thrive Forever</u>? [Play Together; Ultimate Massively Multiplayer; Late Game]

[TOC]

- "Play" – You and our world for our world's future. Ultimate massively multiplayer. Real-life. Real-time. Real people. Real consequences - a surviving and thriving future for all forever.
- Ultimate win - "all thrive forever"
- Setting – the world+ (the world and beyond)

[Web version @ ThriveForever.org]

Why our world <u>can</u> win.

In this "game" and real life, our world <u>can</u> have a surviving and thriving future. To "win" that future, keep in mind that our world has a future already beginning. Whether our future appears bad or good, our world can do better. To build a better future, use Thrive strategy and tools has been used successfully at the personal level and on larger scales (community, country). They can work for the world we all care about. As they have for others, this strategy and these tools can help our world+ build, achieve and sustain a surviving and thriving future.

Why our world <u>must</u> win.

Our world <u>must</u> have a surviving and thriving future. Our world <u>must</u> do better whether our future appears bad or good. Why? Even if we believe that our world has a good future, we are not fully thriving, are not likely to be fully thriving in the future, and are still facing uncertainties about the long term future. We want and need a surviving and thriving future because our world's future is endangered and because of our human need to survive and desire to thrive. What drives our world and all of us is our human need to survive and desire to thrive now and in a sustainable future. Further, because we (past and present) have broken parts of our world and endangered its future, we (present and future) must help fix what is broken and build a survivable and thriving future for our world+.

Why we all must and can win together.

To "win" and build this better future, we (our world's current and future people and leadership) should be partners in this endeavor from the beginning and through each step. Winning depends on positive leadership from us - our world's people and leaders. Winning depends on a collaborative approach where the traditional leaders and the people (also serving as leaders) jointly provide leadership, vision, motivation, strategy and successful execution. A collaborative approach has the greater potential to create and sustain large, positive change and a surviving and thriving world+.

Key to winning is the strong desire by all of us (our world's leaders and people) to move our world+ from its current vulnerabilities through and beyond surviving to a sustained thriving future.

Getting Started.

[TOC]

Getting started with Thrive! – All Thrive Forever "game". [10] Ultimate massively multiplayer. Real-life. Real-time. Real people. Real consequences - a surviving and thriving future for all forever.

1. **Game.** Massively multiplayer (you and our world for our world+).
2. **Mode.** Choose simulation or real-life.
3. **Players.** Choose the team well. Choose other players (non-enemy) and their role, motivation and ability. For each, what is ability, motivation and expected behavior? Specific abilities and motivation lead to greater success in specific roles. Organize team. Make iniitial decision on roles – who will do what when with what resources to produce what result. Make initial decision on how team will play as team (decisions, communication, joint and individual actions).
4. **Game Characters.** You. Simulation and/or real-life characters.
5. **Team Play.** Play as a team. Best if whole team (before and during play) helps make choices ("play", future, path, location, time), draw play map, identify enemies and friends, and explore. Good communication is very important.
6. **Win.** Choose win. Reduce vulnerability. Survive and thrive today, near future, far future. [Use Scoresheet. Win? How well is our world and for how long?] Download fillable scoresheet via ThriveForever.org
7. **Path and Future.** Choose path (Survive, Partial Thrive, and Full Thrive) you will take and future (Survive, Partial Thrive, and Full Thrive) you will seek. Get off Current Path to avoid losing. [See Graphic - Future for Thriving and Surviving]
8. **Play Location.** Choose location best for play and achieving best future. Virtual location (online play). Physical location. Combination is best.
9. **Play Time.** Choose start time. Play real-time with pauses at least for strategy and rest.

---

[10] Free download of larger, fillable scoresheet via ThriveForever.org

10. **"Enemies and Friends"**. Identify real-life friends who help you win. For each, what is ability, motivation and expected behavior? For friends, determine what positive actions each is or will take and why. They may or may not be on your team. Identify real-life enemies who make or keep people vulnerable and/or stop people from surviving and thriving. For each, what is ability, motivation and expected behavior? For enemies, determine what negative actions each is or will take and why. They are defeated when there remain no threats to surviving and thriving.
11. **Environment/Setting.** Our world and its surrounding environment. Pay attention and adjust to changing environment.
12. **Map.** Draw map for play environment. Our world+.
13. **Exploration.** Explore, before and during play, your ever-changing play environment - yourself and our world+ and its internal/external environment. Information gathering helps with strategy, tactics and actions.
14. **Resources.** Identify resources to be used during play. Includes people, things, money that help win.
15. **Obstacles.** Identify obstacles to overcome. These change.
16. **Strategy, Tactics and Actions (Starting).** Having chosen the path (Survive, Partial Thrive, and Full Thrive) you will take and the future (Survive, Partial Thrive, and Full Thrive) you will seek, strategize on how to get off Current Path to avoid losing and get on chosen path to chosen future and win. Strategize. First, near future. Second, far future. Third, forever. Or do simultaneous push for all three.
    - How well should our world+ be in the future?
    - What has to change to achieve our world+'s thriving future?
    - What actions by our world+ are needed to achieve its thriving future?
    - Overall Thrive! strategy and action plan
17. **Adjust above elements as needed during play.**

Play.

[TOC]

Play Thrive! – All Thrive Forever "game" together and win all thrive forever in real life.

1. **Play!** Win near and far future and forever!
2. Execute strategy and tactics.
   - Use Overall Thrive! strategy and action plan
3. Act. Winning?
   - Use Worksheet - Thrive! Strategy & Action Plan. What actions taken? Who did what to/with whom, where, when? With what result?
     - Use Thrive Scoresheet - Win? How well is world+ and for how long? As alternative, you may want to use Thrive (Excel) Scoresheet - Win? How well and for how long? to enter previous information and calculate score. Download fillable scoresheet via ThriveForever.org
4. If winning, congratulations! If losing, do better!
5. Adjust strategies, tactics and actions during play.
6. Pause. Rest?
7. Play! Win!
8. **Win or lose, continue "game".** This is real life.
9. **Play!** Win surviving and thriving future. **Ultimate score is 150,000!**
   - See Graphic - Thrive Score: Winning? Thriving?

5. Path and Future. *[Back]*

During "play", you and all of us face four possible futures [See Graphic - Future for Thriving and Surviving]:

- Current Path where there is little thriving and survival ends much too soon. Loss.
- Survive Path where there is little thriving and survival is extended but still ends too soon. Smaller loss.
- Partial Thrive Path where there is more thriving and survival is extended more but still ends too soon. Partial win.
- Full Thrive Path where there is high thriving and survival is extended to maximum. Ultimate win.

To avoid losing, get off Current Path. For ultimate win, get on Full Thrive Path where you and all of us survive and thrive today, near and far future, and forever.

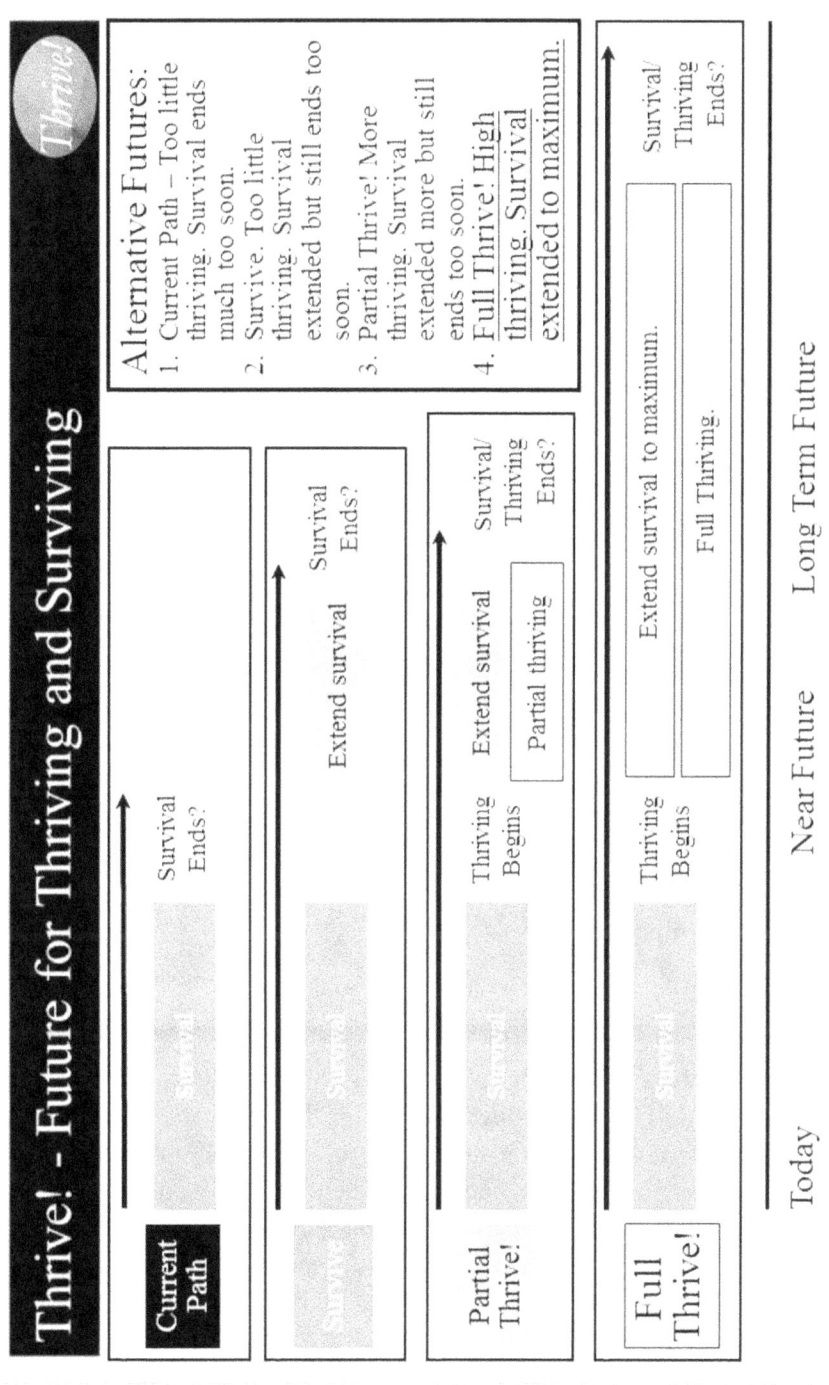

Graphic - Future for Thriving and Surviving

What should our world+ be and how well in the future? *[Back]*

What should our world+ be in the future? How well should our world+ as a whole be in the future? Overall, it should be <u>surviving and thriving</u>. With this as a guide, you and our world+ choose the surviving and thriving future our world+ wants to build and achieve.

To "win", our world and our people should be:
- performing (living, working, recreating, learning) well enough to survive and thrive.
- well-off (financially) enough to survive and thrive.
- well nourished (food and drink) enough to survive and thrive.
- well housed enough to survive and thrive.
- well protected (exposures, crime) enough to survive and thrive.
- well educated enough to survive and thrive.
- physically and mentally well enough to survive and thrive.
- personally growing/developing well enough to survive and thrive.
- in good habitat enough to survive and thrive.
- not vulnerable.
- producing personal and public goods enough to survive and thrive.
- in a stable, positive climate.
- sustained.

Use <u>Worksheet - What should your world be and how well?</u> to describe how well our world+ should be. From you and our world's view and to be surviving and thriving, indicate to what extent our world+ should be performing well. Be well-off (financially). Be well nourished (food and drink). Be well housed. Be well protected (exposures, crime). Be well educated. Be physically and mentally well. Be personally growing/developing well. Be living within good habitat. Not be vulnerable. Be producing personal and public goods. Be living within a stable, positive climate. Be sustained. Again, our world+ should be surviving and thriving.

Thriving and Surviving	What should our world+ be and how well (not surviving, surviving, thriving) in the future?
Performing (live/work/play) well?	
Well-off?	
Well nourished?	
Well housed?	
Well protected?	
Well educated?	
Physically/ mentally well?	
Growing/ developing well?	
Living in good habitat?	
Not vulnerable?	
Producing personal/ public goods?	
Stable, positive climate?	
Sustainable?	

Worksheet - What should our world+ be and how well?

What has to change externally and internally to achieve our world+'s thriving future? *[Back]*

What has to change externally (outside our world) and internally (within our world) to progress from our world's current status to achieve desired surviving and thriving status? You identified what positively and negatively impacts or is likely to impact our world+. Update those, including any changes to your future world+.

Given those, what has to change to achieve a surviving and thriving future? Use Worksheet - Thrive! Strategy and Action Plan. What changes needed? to describe all that has to change externally and internally.

Good changes improve and/or sustain surviving and thriving. Bad changes prevent and/or limit surviving and thriving.

Thriving and Surviving	Changes needed to achieve surviving and thriving future
Performing (live/ work/play) well?	
Well-off?	
Well nourished?	
Well housed?	
Well protected?	
Well educated?	
Physically/ mentally well?	
Growing/ developing well?	
Living in good habitat?	
Not vulnerable?	
Producing personal/public goods?	
Stable, positive climate?	
Sustainable?	

Worksheet - *Thrive!* Strategy and Action Plan. What changes needed?

-

What actions by our world+ are needed to achieve its thriving future? *[Back]*

What actions are needed to bring about needed changes that improve our world+ to achieve surviving and thriving status? [See Graphic - What will Thrive! Endeavor, you and the world, do so all thrive forever?]

Very important actions are needed. Individual world+ members and our world+ as a whole should support our strategy. Use Worksheet - Thrive! Strategy and Action Plan. What actions needed?

Identify actions by our world+ that support good changes that will help improve and/or sustain surviving and thriving. If good changes are likely to occur, support them. If good changes are not likely to occur, support them and develop other good changes to compensate.

Identify actions by our world+ that stop bad changes that prevent or limit surviving and thriving. If bad changes are not likely to occur, ensure they do not. If bad changes are likely to occur, change them, stop them or avoid/reduce their impact.

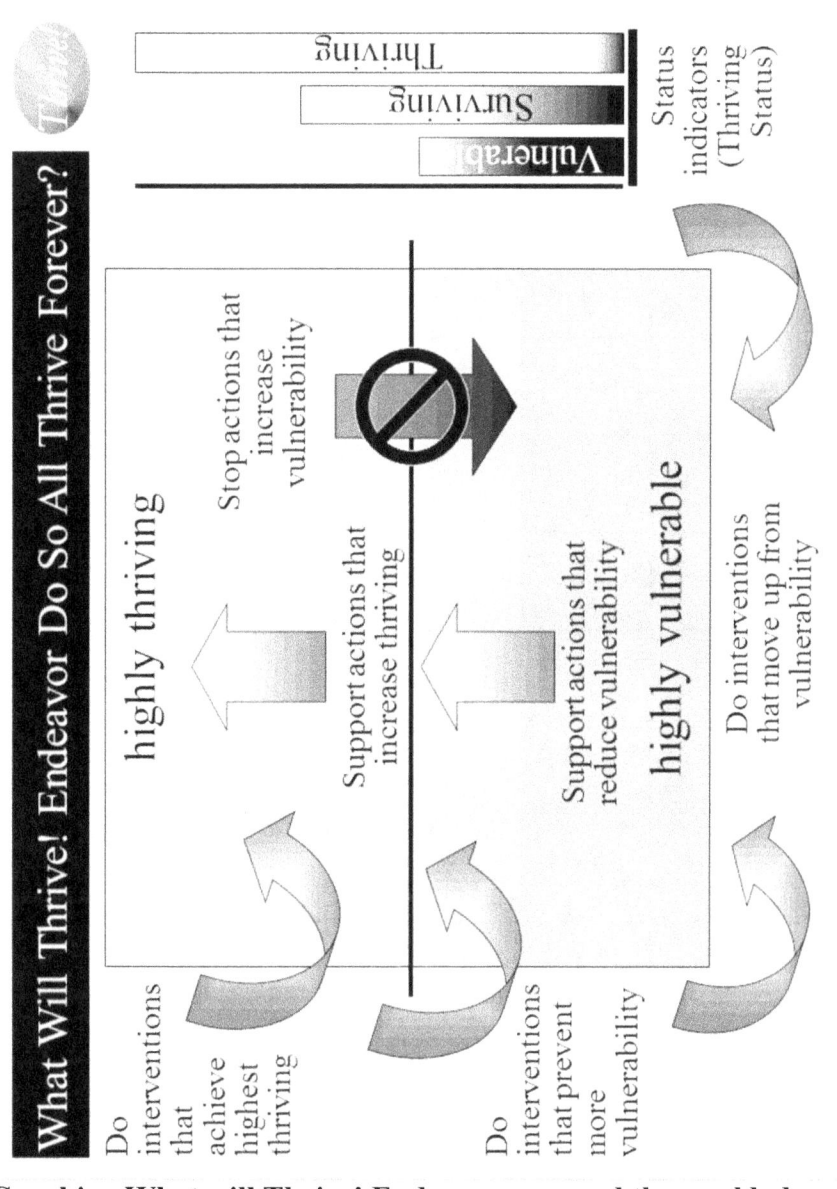

Graphic - What will Thrive! Endeavor, you and the world, do so all thrive forever?

Thriving and Surviving	Actions - Who will do what to/with whom, where, when, and with what result?
Performing (live/work/play) well?	
Well-off?	
Well nourished?	
Well housed?	
Well protected?	
Well educated?	
Physically/mentally well?	
Growing/developing well?	
Living in good habitat?	
Not vulnerable?	
Producing personal/public goods?	
Stable, positive climate?	
Sustainable?	

Worksheet - *Thrive!* Strategy and Action Plan. What actions needed?

Overall Thrive! strategy and action plan. *[Back]*

Your overall *Thrive!* strategy, tactics and actions will be our world's *Thrive!* **Strategy and Action Plan**. [11] Different members of our world+ will take on different responsibilities. For each action, designate who of our world+ will do what to/with whom, where, when, with what resources and with what result. Use Worksheet - Actions: Who, what, whom, when, where, resources, result to document detailed actions and responsibilities. Make sure you have all actions needed to build, achieve and sustain a surviving and thriving world+.

As the strategy is executed, your strategy, actions and results should be updated in your *Thrive!* **Strategy and Action Plan**.

Periodically, you and our world+ should assess your strategies/actions near and long term impact on near and long term surviving and thriving. When a) your strategies and actions are not building and sustaining a thriving future and/or b) there are changes in the world or its surrounding environment, adjust your *Thrive!* **Strategy and Action Plan**.

Successfully execute your world's *Thrive!* **Strategy and Action Plan** and to build a near and long term surviving and thriving future. Each and all must successfully carry out the assigned action and do what is required to/with whoever is required, where required, when required, and with what needed/desired result. A *Thrive!* **Strategy and Action Plan** is only as good as its successful execution and successful achievement of the desired outcome - a surviving and thriving future. *[Following is an example of **Thrive! Strategy and Action Plan** for you and our world's surviving and thriving future.]*

---

[11] To win and build a surviving and thriving future for you and our world+, Thrive can be helpful to you. The **Thrive! Next Generation Toolkit** is laid out in the full **People's Guide** and in ***Thrive! - Building a Thriving Future*** - a manual providing greater depth on strategy and tools and available via Amazon.com or free download from ThrivingFuture.org.

Who	Does What	To/With Whom	When	Where	With What Resources	With What Result

Worksheet - Actions: Who, what, whom, when, where, resources, result.

Example of our world surviving and thriving. To build, achieve and sustain a surviving *and* thriving future, the **Thrive! Strategy and Action Plan** *for you and our world+ should be more like the following example: [Who will do what to/with whom, where, when, with what resources with what result?]*

Starting immediately, we (people, business/industry, private organizations (local, country), governments (local, country) and international organizations) build, achieve, and sustain a surviving and thriving future for our world and for all forever, including:
- Performing well. *Starting immediately, people, business/industry, private organizations (local, country), governments (local, country) and international organizations act to ensure, within the next 20 years, a) all (who are able and not appropriately retired) can work and earn a living income sufficient to survive and thrive and b) all have sufficient resources for and are living, recreating, learning so that they are surviving and thriving to maximum extent feasible.*
- Being well-off (financially). *Starting immediately, people, business/industry, private organizations (local, country), governments (local, country) and international organizations act to ensure, within the next 20 years, a) all have sufficient income/resources to survive and thrive and b) all governments have sufficient resources to provide needed (supporting surviving) and desired (supporting thriving) public programs and policies.*
- Being well nourished (food and drink). *Starting immediately, people, business/industry, private organizations (local, country), governments (local, country) and international organizations act to ensure, within the next 20 years, that all people have access to, be able to afford and consume healthy foods enough to survive and thrive.*
- Being well housed. *Starting immediately, people, business/industry, private organizations (local, country), governments (local, country) and international organizations act to ensure, within the next 20 years, all have access to, be able to afford and live in adequate and preferably high performing housing that supports surviving and thriving.*
- Being well protected (exposures, crime). *Starting immediately, people, business/industry, private organizations (local, country),*

governments (local, country) and international organizations act to ensure, within the next 20 years, a) environmental exposures in home, workplace and elsewhere are minimized so as to not prevent surviving and thriving and b) crimes are minimized to the extent feasible in terms of frequency and impact so as to not prevent surviving and thriving.

- Being well educated. *Starting immediately, people, business/industry, private organizations (local, country), governments (local, country) and international organizations act to ensure, within the next 20 years, all people are educated to the full extent of their abilities, needs and desires and to support their surviving and thriving.*

- Being physically and mentally well. *Starting immediately, people, business/industry, private organizations (local, country), governments (local, country) and international organizations act to ensure, within the next 20 years, a) all people receive the optimal health support to ensure, within the next 20 years, surviving and thriving and b) all people's physical and mental health is optimized to best ensure surviving and thriving.*

- Personally growing/developing well. *Starting immediately, people, business/industry, private organizations (local, country), governments (local, country) and international organizations act to ensure, within the next 20 years, all people are personally growing and developing to best ensure surviving and thriving.*

- Living within good habitat. *Starting immediately, people, business/industry, private organizations (local, country), governments (local, country) and international organizations act to ensure, within the next 20 years, a) all people have access to habitat that best supports their surviving and thriving and b) our world has the optimal mix, quantity and quality of habitat to best support our world and its inhabitants' surviving and thriving.*

- Not being vulnerable. *Starting immediately, people, business/industry, private organizations (local, country), governments (local, country) and international organizations act to ensure, within the next 20 years, our world and all of its people, if vulnerable, are vulnerable only to the minimum extent feasible.*

- Producing personal and public goods. *Starting immediately, people, business/industry, private organizations (local, country), governments (local, country) and international organizations act to ensure, within the next 20 years, our people produce personal and public goods (including personal income/resources, housing, food and drink, energy, education, health, protection, personal growth and development, and habitat) so as to support surviving and thriving for all persons and for our world overall.*

- Living within a stable, positive climate. *Starting immediately, people, business/industry, private organizations (local, country), governments (local, country) and international organizations act to ensure, within the next 10 years, all people behave so as to avoid negative impacts and support positive impacts so as to help ensure a stable, positive climate.*

- Being sustained. *Starting immediately, people, business/industry, private organizations (local, country), governments (local, country) and international organizations act to ensure, within the next 5 years, all people behave so as to ensure the sustainability of our world <u>and</u> its people.*

Worksheet - *Thrive!* Strategy & Action Plan. What actions taken?

Thriving and Surviving	Actions - Who <u>did</u> what to/with whom, where, when, and with what result?
Performing (live/ work/play) well?	
Well-off?	
Well nourished?	
Well housed?	
Well protected?	
Well educated?	
Physically/ mentally well?	
Growing/ developing well?	
Living in good habitat?	
Not vulnerable?	
Producing personal/public goods?	
Stable, positive climate?	
Sustainable?	

Scoresheet - Win? How well is world+ and for how long?

* Near – less than 5 years. Far – 5-100 years. Forever – more than 100 years.

Thriving and Surviving	How well? Not survive? Survive? Thrive? [Pick one] _0 NotS 50 Survive 100 Thrive	How long? * Near future? Far future? Forever? [Pick one] _25 Near _75 Far 100 Forever	Score [How well x How long]
Performing (live/ work/play) well?			
Well-off?			
Well nourished?			
Well housed?			
Well protected?			
Well educated?			
Physically/ mentally well?			
Growing/ developing well?			
Living in good habitat?			
Not vulnerable?			
Producing personal /public goods?			
Stable, positive climate?			
Sustainable?			
		Bonus – if 10,000 on all, add 20,000	
		Total Win Ultimate - 150,000	

Thrive (Excel) Scoresheet - Win? How well and for how long?

Download fillable scoresheet via ThriveForever.org

Graphic - Thrive Score: Winning? Thriving?

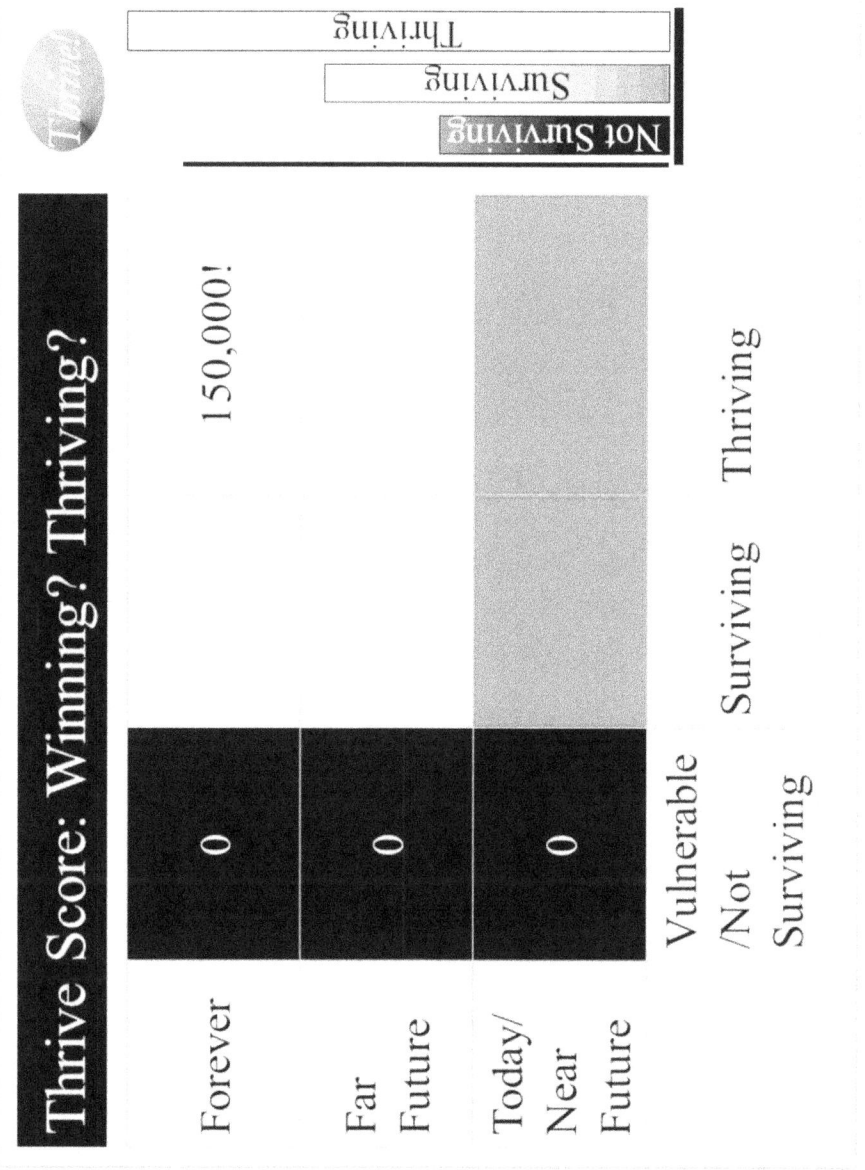

www.ingramcontent.com/pod-product-compliance
Lightning Source LLC
Chambersburg PA
CBHW070755290526
45795CB00002B/559